Dying to Reach God

Dying to Reach God

A New Translation and Commentary on the Writings
of St. Ignatius of Antioch and St. Polycarp of Smyrna,
Second-Century Christian Martyrs

William W. Weber

RESOURCE *Publications* · Eugene, Oregon

DYING TO REACH GOD
A New Translation and Commentary on the Writings of St. Ignatius of Antioch
and St. Polycarp of Smyrna, Second-Century Christian Martyrs

Resource Publications
An Imprint of Wipf and Stock Publishers
199 W. 8th Ave., Suite 3
Eugene, OR 97401

www.wipfandstock.com

PAPERBACK ISBN: 978-1-6667-7575-4
HARDCOVER ISBN: 978-1-6667-7576-1
EBOOK ISBN: 978-1-6667-7577-8

VERSION NUMBER 07/25/24

To my loving wife
and boon companion, Lindsey:
Much Thanks and Many Years!

To our departed son, Joseph Nicholas Weber,
our departed godson, Brian Symeon Valentine,
and our departed friend, Rose Koury,
who was the inspiration for this work:
Memory Eternal!

To our family patron and helper,
St. Ephraim of Nea Makri,
Great Martyr and Wonderworker,
who ever pours forth God's grace
on those who earnestly beseech him:
Much Thanks!

My passionate desire has been crucified,
and there is in me no fire of love
burning for material things.
Rather there is water
living and speaking in me,
saying to me from within,
"Come to the Father."

St. Ignatius of Antioch
The Epistle to the Romans 7.2

I bless you because you have counted me worthy
of this day and hour to receive a place
among the number of the martyrs
in the cup of your Christ,
and thus to share
in the resurrection
to eternal life,
both of soul and of body,
in the incorruptibility of the Holy Spirit.
May I be admitted among them
in your presence today
as a sacrifice that is fat and acceptable,
just as you prepared beforehand,
showed in advance, and have brought to fulfilment,
O never-lying and truthful God.

St. Polycarp of Smyrna
The Martyrdom of St. Polycarp 14.2

Contents

Acknowledgments

THERE ARE MANY I wish to recognize. My father for taking me to Sunday school and church. My teachers in Greek, Hebrew, and Latin, especially Dr. Gerry Miller, Rev. Dr. William Coker, Dr. Hubert Martin, and Dr. Jane Phillips. Dr. Mark Elliott for introducing me to the practice of scholarly writing, the Russian Orthodox Church, and icons. Kent Ostrander for urging me to finish my Master of Arts in History and Dr. John Scarborough for insisting my master's thesis be ready to defend by a specific date. His Grace Bishop BASIL (Essey) for receiving our family into the Orthodox Church. Rose Koury for inspiring me to write this book and our son Austin for his support in bringing this book to publication. Father Alexis Kouri for blessing this undertaking. Protopresbyter Dr. Gregory Wingenbach and Dr. James Sigountos for critiquing my Greek translations and commentary. Dr. Carmen Hardin for reviewing my Latin translation of St. Polycarp. Dr. JohnMark Beazley for challenging me to engage the scholarly literature more fully. Brian Brooks for making the map and Brian Whirledge for writing the icons of St. Ignatius and St. Polycarp. Michael Stoddard for technical assistance. Richard Johnson for his singular service. All those whose translations, commentaries, books, and articles made this book possible. All our Christian brothers and sisters who have carried us through the loss of our son Joseph. And my wonderful bride of over forty years, Lindsey, my joy, whose loving support remains beyond description. Any mistakes in this book reflect on me alone. For whatever may be of use, to God be the glory!

A Few Words on Translations

THE SEPTUAGINT (LXX) IS the Greek translation of the Old Testament quoted often, but not always, by Christ and his apostles. St. Ignatius and St. Polycarp used it, and the Orthodox Church continues to use it. The Masoretic Text (MT) is the final form of the Hebrew text of the Old Testament finished by Jewish rabbis about nine hundred years after Christ. Most translations of the Old Testament are based on it.

The order of the Old Testament books used in the Abbreviations section of this book is that found in modern editions of the LXX. 4 Maccabees, which the LXX has as an appendix, is cited because its material is important for Christian martyrdom. The abbreviations LXX and MT are only included in scripture references where their texts differ or when the verses cited are a direct quotation of the LXX. Where chapter numbers differ between the LXX and MT, the LXX is given first (for example, Psalm 15/16:10). Where the verse numbers differ in the Orthodox Study Bible, this is also noted.

Where scripture is quoted, the translation is that of the author. https://www.Biblehub.com is an excellent site for finding other translations for any given scripture. The scriptures cited in the commentaries and three introductions represent only a portion of the partial quotes and innumerable allusions used by Ignatius, Polycarp, and the author of *The Martyrdom of St. Polycarp*. The references are provided as an aid to reflection and further study. Please note that all translations of Patristic texts, such as those of St. Irenaeus of Lyons, are also those of the author.

Key to the Format of this Work

WHEN THE READER OPENS this book to the translated texts, the translation is on the left and the commentary is on the right. In the commentary, words in **boldface** type are from the translated text, while words in *italics* are usually alternate translations, although occasionally they may represent Greek or Latin words or are used in other, ordinary ways. For example, the commentary on Ephesians 20.1 includes the following:

> We have no **second work** from Ignatius to the Ephesians. Nor do we have another instance of his using the Greek word *oikonomia*, rendered here and in 18.2 as "**plan of salvation**." *Oikonomia* is traditionally translated *economy* or *dispensation* and includes God's **plan** (or *arrangement*) and its *management*.

Abbreviations

IN THIS BOOK, SCRIPTURE references have a colon (:) between chapter and verse, while patristic citations have a period (.). Thus, Rom 6:1 refers to the Bible, while Rom 6.1 refers to St. Ignatius's *Epistle to the Romans*. This is also how one can tell whether *The Epistle to the Ephesians* (Eph) is the one by St. Paul or by St. Ignatius and whether *The Epistle to the Philippians* (Phil) is the one by St. Paul or by St. Polycarp.

The following abbreviations are used:

cf.	compare
ed.	edition
fn.	footnote
fnn.	footnotes
Intro	Introduction
LXX	Septuagint (Greek Old Testament)
MT	Masoretic Text (Hebrew Old Testament)
OSB	Orthodox Study Bible
p.	page
pp.	pages
Gen	Genesis
Exod	Exodus
Lev	Leviticus
Num	Numbers
Deut	Deuteronomy
Josh	Joshua
Judg	Judges
1 Kgdms	1 Kingdoms (LXX title)
= 1 Sam	1 Samuel (MT title)
4 Kgdms	4 Kingdoms (LXX title)

= 2 Kgs	2 Kings (MT title)
2 Chr	2 Chronicles
Tob	Tobit
2 Macc	2 Maccabees
3 Macc	3 Maccabees
Ps	Psalm
Prov	Proverbs
Wis	Wisdom of Solomon
Sir	Wisdom of Sirach (Ecclesiasticus)
Mal	Malachi
Isa	Isaiah
Ezek	Ezekiel
Dan	Daniel
4 Macc	4 Maccabees
Matt	Matthew
Acts	Acts of the Apostles
Rom	Romans
1 Cor	1 Corinthians
2 Cor	2 Corinthians
Gal	Galatians
Eph	Ephesians
Phil	Philippians
Col	Colossians
1 Thess	1 Thessalonians
2 Thess	2 Thessalonians
1 Tim	1 Timothy
2 Tim	2 Timothy
Phlm	Philemon
Heb	Hebrews
Jas	James
1 Pet	1 Peter
2 Pet	2 Peter
Rev	Revelation
Eph	Ephesians (Ignatius)
Mag	Magnesians (Ignatius)
Tr	Trallians (Ignatius)

Rom	Romans (Ignatius)
Phld	Philadelphians (Ignatius)
Sm	Smyrnaeans (Ignatius)
Pol	Polycarp (Ignatius)
Phil	Philippians (Polycarp)
Mart Pol	Martyrdom of Polycarp
Mosc	Moscow Manuscript
Sal	Salutation
Ag Heresies	Against Heresies (Irenaeus)
Apost Const	Apostolic Constitutions
Apost Trad	Apostolic Tradition (Hippolytus)
Barn	Epistle of Barnabas
Ch Hist	Church History (Eusebius)
Chron	Chronicon (Eusebius)
1 Clem	1 Clement (Clement)
2 Clem	2 Clement (Anonymous)
Confess	Confession (Patrick)
Convers	Conversation with Motovilov (Seraphim of Sarov)
Dem	Demonstration of the Apostolic Preaching (Irenaeus)
Dialog 1	Dialogue 1, The Immutable (Theodoret)
Did	Didache (also titled, Teaching of the Twelve Apostles)
Diogn	Epistle to Diognetus
Frag	Fragments (Irenaeus)
Hom Ign	Homily on Ignatius (John Chrysostom)
Lives	Lives of Illustrious Men (Jerome)
Mart Ign	Martyrdom of Ignatius
Mart Pion	Martyrdom of Pionius
Misc	Miscellanies (Stromateis) (Clement of Alexandria)
Life Pol	Life of Polycarp (Pionius)
Prescript	Prescription against Heretics (Tertullian)
Prov	Proverbs (Zenobius)

Introduction

ST. IGNATIUS AND ST. Polycarp were influential bishops and martyrs of the second-century Church. From Ignatius, we have seven epistles that he wrote on his way to martyrdom in Rome. In the case of Polycarp, we have his epistle to the church at Philippi, which St. Paul founded, as well as a detailed narrative of his martyrdom written soon after his death. While these writings have been translated before and commentaries and studies abound, their observations are often long on academic detail and short on piety. There is a great need for a translation and commentary within the Orthodox Christian tradition that can be used devotionally by Christians from many faith traditions, one that encourages and exhorts them to learn from the words and deeds of these great saints how to follow Christ in the apostolic way of sacrificial and submissive love.

The translations in this book have been specially crafted to aid memorization, and the reader is invited to read them aloud and reflect on them. Such pondering mirrors the internalizing of the gospel by St. Ignatius and St. Polycarp.[1] Professor Vall says that Ignatius's epistles "are inherently geared toward theological reflection on, and elaboration of, the mystery of Christ."[2] It could be said that Polycarp's epistle is a reflection on and application of "Christ Jesus" as "our righteousness" (Phil 8.1, 3.1).

I owe an incalculable debt to Professor Vall for his stellar study: *Learning Christ: Ignatius of Antioch and the Mystery of Redemption.* While clearly acknowledging the value of the historical-critical method, Vall does more than just utilize it as he goes beyond it to plumb the depths of the saint's understanding of our redemption. The "intention" of Ignatius, Vall writes, "is not only to get across his ideas but also that his readers would consider

---

1. St. Irenaeus, the disciple of St. Polycarp, says of himself that he was still "ruminating" on the words of Polycarp decades after knowing him (see Polycarp Intro, 159, fn. 20).

2. Vall, *Learning Christ*, 18.

these realities for themselves, view them in a new light, enter more deeply into them, or act on them in a specific way. . . .in order to ponder with him the matter at hand: the mystery of Jesus Christ and all that it entails."[3] Ignatius's epistles, he explains, "are meant to be interactive and are composed to elicit a whole range of responses in the reader. This hermeneutical observation stands in considerable tension with the ideal of disinterested historical neutrality, especially when it comes to the study of texts of a religious or theological nature."[4] Though trained as a historian, I recognize that there are limits to applying the canons of modern historiography to the texts of St. Ignatius and St. Polycarp. To be clear, academic commentaries and articles that employ the methods of higher criticism can be helpful, and Vall's treatise and this volume make regular use of them. Furthermore, the translations in this book are academically rigorous, taking into account prior translations and being undergirded by historical, linguistic, and theological study. However—and this is the point—scholarly scrutiny of patristic texts without personal reflection and application is insufficient.

Consequently, this book includes various tools for study of and reflection upon these texts, so the reader may apply them. There are separate introductions for both Ignatius and Polycarp, commentary on the texts, and an annotated bibliography. Citations of secondary sources are mostly confined to the introductions on Ignatius and Polycarp. Readers who are interested in the scholarly literature will find the works and bibliographies of Holmes, Schoedel, Vall, and Hartog—which are referenced in the annotated bibliographies—to be a good place to begin their investigation. Occasionally, in the commentary sections, the reader is given some idea of scholarly opinions about a matter being discussed without the names and works of scholars being cited. To quote them would go beyond the scope of this book. What does get cited repeatedly in the commentaries is what is central for reflection and application. Thus they are full of intertextual references to the nine texts in this volume, contain copious citations of scripture, and include a number of patristic references. These have been placed within parentheses so the reader can look at them immediately or skip over them until later. In addition, comments cover historical, geographical, and linguistic matters, all the while considering Jesus Christ, the mystery of

3. Vall, *Learning Christ*, 7 (for more on this, see 85–87). Vall lays out the details of his methodological approach in pp. 1–23.

4. Vall, *Learning Christ*, 9. At times, Ignatius's grammar intentionally fosters multiple understandings that are all valid.

redemption, and how we may partake of him. The reader should look over the pages on translations, formatting, and abbreviations, before proceeding to the texts and their accompanying commentary.

This volume is presented with the hope and prayer that the writings and martyrdoms of these great saints will stir up all of us to lay aside our individualistic wants and ways, forsake the vanity of this world, put our sinful passions to death, and live our lives together in and for Christ, so that having proved to be his disciples, we may in the end reach God.

St. Ignatius of Antioch

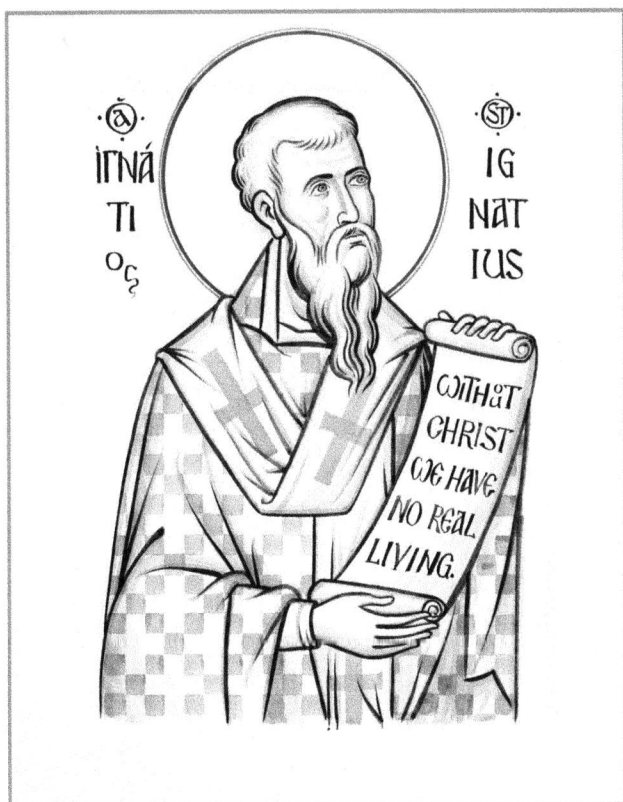

Ignatios
ST Ignatius

Without Christ we have no real living.

Introduction to St. Ignatius

ST. IGNATIUS RANKS AS one of the three most influential bishops and teachers of the second-century Christian Church. He provides a direct link from the apostles—especially St. John—to the other two, St. Polycarp of Smyrna and St. Irenaeus of Lyons.

Ignatius, according to St. John Chrysostom, knew many of the apostles personally; and he was ordained by them as the second bishop of Antioch after its first bishop, St. Evodius, died around the year 69.[1] He went on to serve in Antioch for some forty years.[2] Furthermore, the Orthodox *Synaxarion* says, "Ignatius had known the apostles in his youth and, in company with Polycarp, was initiated into the deepest mysteries of the faith by St. John."[3] The churches that St. John wrote to at Ephesus, Smyrna, and Philadelphia (Rev 2–3) were later written to by Ignatius. The Ephesian church had previously received an epistle from St. Paul. Scholars have noted the influence of St. Paul, St. John, and St. Matthew on Ignatius.[4] "Ignatius's theology," Vall says, "combines Pauline, Johannine, and Matthean elements. In particular, his distinctive insight into the mystery

---

1. Hom Ign 1–2, Ch Hist 3.22, Chron 2. His appointment or ordination as bishop is variously attributed to St. Peter (by Theodoret, Dialog 1), St. Paul (Apost Const 7.46), and St. John (Coptic Synaxarium. Kiahk 24). Although St. Peter and St. Paul died under Nero (who died in in the year 68), they could have been involved in Ignatius's selection before he took office (on Polycarp's selection, see Polycarp Intro, 158, fnn. 6–7). The Apostle John may have been the one who actually ordained him bishop.

2. Until at least 107. For the year of his death, see Ignatius Intro, 5, fn. 8.

3. *The Synaxarion of Holy Hieromartyr Ignatius the God-Bearer of Antioch. December 20.*

4. Grant, *Ignatius of Antioch*, 1–3; Schoedel, *Ignatius of Antioch*, 9–10; Vall, *Learning Christ*, 1, 40–49, 125, 128, 164, 232.

of redemption synthesizes an essentially Johannine understanding of the incarnation with the Pauline theme of suffering with Christ."[5]

The martyrdom of St. Stephen in Jerusalem by the Jews brought persecution, and some of the faithful that were scattered by it found their way to the great city of Antioch-on-the-Orontes in Syria. Only Alexandria and Rome itself were more important to the Roman Empire. At first the word was just preached to Jews, but then Gentiles heard about the Lord Jesus "and a great number believed and turned to the Lord" (Acts 11:21). The church at Jerusalem then sent out Barnabas, who brought Paul along. Together they taught the faithful in Antioch for a whole year. "And the disciples were first called Christians at Antioch" (11:26). Another first for Antioch occurred when her bishop, St. Ignatius, penned the term *Christianity*, which had not been seen before (Magn 10.1, 3; Rom 3.3; Phld 6.1).

It was from Antioch that Barnabas and Paul were sent forth to preach the gospel (Acts 13:1–3). And it was to Antioch they returned, where they "recounted all that God had done with them and how he had opened a door of faith for the Gentiles" (14:27). There also they were accosted by Judaizing Christians.[6] These men insisted that the Gentiles must be circumcised and keep the entire law of Moses, in order for them to be saved (15:1, 5). So the apostles and elders (presbyters) held council in Jerusalem and in agreement with the input of Paul and Barnabas and Peter declared that salvation comes by faith "through the grace of the Lord Jesus Christ" (15:11, 9). Nevertheless, sharing meals between Jewish Christians who sought to keep a kosher diet and Gentiles who did not would be a lingering issue (Gal 2:1–21, especially 11–14). Ignatius himself would have to deal with problems with Judaizers in his epistles (see Mag 8–11 and Phld 2–9 in particular).

Our sources for St. Ignatius are limited. Most important are his seven epistles, which have long been accepted as genuine in their shorter, noninterpolated form. He wrote them as he traveled through the Roman province of Asia on his way to martyrdom. In the early second century, the state was not actively persecuting Christians, and arrest and conviction

---

5. Vall, *Learning Christ*, 125.

6. *To Judaize* means to live like a Jew or compel others to do so. It is used twice in the Bible (Esther 8:17 LXX, Gal 2:14). Judaizers stressed being circumcised (Esther 8:17 LXX; Acts 15:1, 5; Col 2:11; Phil 3:2–7; Phld 6.1), following a kosher diet (Acts 15:5, Gal 2:1–15, Col 2:16), keeping the Sabbath (Col 2:16, Mag 9.1, Phld 4.1, Matt 12:8), and approaching scripture like a Jew (Phld 8.2). There were some Jewish Christians, called Nazarenes, who sought to keep the law themselves without compelling Gentile believers to do so (Acts 21:17–26, 24:5; On Isaiah 8:14).

just for bearing the name of Christian was contrary to imperial policy.[7] Thus Ignatius could receive delegations from churches without endangering those involved (Eph 1.2–3, 2.1; Mag 2.1, 15.1; Tr 1.1, 12.1, 13.1; Rom 9.3, 10.1; Phld 11.2; Sm 12.1), and Christians were able to collect the bones of their martyrs (Mart Pol 17.1—18.2). But Christianity was still illegal, and if Christians were brought before the authorities, they would be given three chances to recant and offer incense to the gods—which included the emperor—or face execution (see St. Polycarp's case in Mart Pol 8.1—12.2).

Regarding Ignatius's own situation, the church historian Eusebius records that the saint was martyred in Rome under the emperor Trajan.[8] Some speculate he was born as early as the year 30, based on the tradition that he was the young child that Jesus picked up and blessed in *Matthew* 18:1–4.[9, 10] For specifics about Ignatius's arrest, confession, condemnation, and martyrdom, we have the *Acts of the Martyrdom of St. Ignatius*.[11] This text claims to be the work of eyewitnesses to his death, but its composition may have been completed several centuries later. Even so, the text does contain valuable oral tradition and some of the details found in it are also found in the Orthodox *Synaxarion*, which is another important source for personal information surrounding his arrest and martyrdom.

The story begins with Trajan issuing an edict for everyone to offer sacrifices to the pagan gods.[12] As the emperor passes through Antioch, the

7. Frend, *Martyrdom and Persecution*, 162–67. This policy is set forth in letters written in 112 between the governor Pliny and the emperor Trajan. A date for Ignatius's arrest after these letters fits well with his circumstances and with a possible death in 114, the year Trajan came to Antioch. The emperor could have sentenced St. Ignatius to death, but sent him on to Rome as a convict under military guard for execution there, in order to avoid leaving trouble behind if he made him a martyr in Antioch before setting out on his campaigns against Armenia and Parthia (cf. Mart Ign 1–2).

8. Ch Hist 3.21–22, Chron 2, Rom 10.3. Many scholars question Eusebius's date of 107/108 for Ignatius's martyrdom, but most accept he died under Trajan (between 98 and 117 inclusive). His *Martyrdom* indicates a death in 114 (see Ignatius Intro, 5, fn. 7).

9. *Prologue from Ochrid*: The Hieromartyr Ignatius the God-Bearer, Bishop of Antioch. December 20th. God-borne (referring to Ignatius being picked up by our Lord) becomes God-bearer by a change in the placement of the Greek accent. This shift reflects Ignatius's lifelong growth in partaking of God (cf. Eph 4.2).

10. By saying that Ignatius "was raised alongside [the apostles] and went everywhere in their company," Chrysostom supports a birth for him in the early 30s of the first century (Hom Ign 1).

11. There is an Antiochene and a Roman version. We will draw from the former in the paragraph that follows.

12. Mart Ign 2.

saint comes before him, wishing to save his flock by laying down his own life for them (Hom Ign 1; also see John 10:11, 1 John 3:16, Tr 13.3). Otherwise a catastrophe will ensue, with many being put to death and others denying Christ. Trajan exclaims, "Who are you, you ill-fated demoniac?" and the fiery Ignatius (for *fiery* is said to be the meaning of his name) retorts, "Nobody calls the God-bearer an ill-fated demoniac!" Trajan taunts him, "Who is a god-bearer?" and Ignatius replies, "One who has Christ in his heart." Then Trajan maligns Christ, "You mean the one who was crucified under Pontius Pilate?" And Ignatius proclaims, "The one who nailed sin, with its originator, to the cross, and sentenced demonic malice to be trampled underfoot by those who carry him in their heart." Finally Trajan asks, "So you carry Christ in your heart?" and Ignatius confesses, "Indeed I do!" Trajan then has Ignatius put in chains and sent off to Rome to be fed to the wild beasts. The emperor thinks he has won, but the saint has been given what he wants.

Modern man does not understand the mind of the saints. Those who love themselves, how can they comprehend someone who loves Christ to death? Ignatius exclaimed,

> I of my own free will am dying for God. Let me be the food of wild beasts; through them I can attain to God. (Rom 4.1)

> Come upon me fire and cross, packs of wild beasts, mutilations, rendings, wrenching of my bones, hacking of my limbs to pieces, repeated grinding of my whole body, cruel tortures of the Devil— only let me attain to Jesus Christ! (Rom 5.3)

The expression *dying to* poignantly conveys St. Ignatius's spiritual and emotional longing and eagerness to reach God. Such a heart's devotion cries out to be literally fulfilled by the saint physically *dying to reach God*. How can we "know what is best" or "normal" for him in such circumstances? How can we the insane judge the sane? Having been swallowed up by his love for God, the *Synaxarion* records that St. Ignatius will go on to be devoured by ravenous lions and thereby attain to God. May his example kindle in us an ardent desire that leaves "no fire of love burning for material things" (Rom 7.2), but only the "passionate desire" to "seek him who died on our behalf," to "want him who rose for our sakes" (Rom 7.2, 6.1).

St. Ignatius is a fervent example of a life lived in union with Christ, "without" whom "we have no real living" (Tr 9.2). He is also a passionate voice for Christian unity. Through the Apostle John he had learned of

Christ's prayer for all of us to "be one" (John 17:20–23, Eph 2.2, Mag 1.2). As he wrote to the Ephesians, "It is profitable, then, for you to be in blameless unity, so that you may also and always be partaking of God" (4.2). When you are in "harmonious unity" with the leaders of your churches and all your fellow members (5.1), then your weekly gathering together to "celebrate God's Eucharist and bring glory to him" will "cast down the powers of Satan" and undo "his destructiveness by your unanimity in the faith" (13.1).

This unity stretches across centuries to include "Abraham and Isaac and Jacob and the prophets and the apostles and the Church" (Phld 9.1). What St. Ignatius calls this unity is the Catholic Church, and he is the first on record to put this term down in writing (see Sm 8.2 and accompanying comments on the term *Catholic Church*). This unity excludes the heretics.

> Therefore, I exhort you: avail yourselves of only Christian fare, and avoid any strange plant, which is heresy. (Tr 6.1)
>
> Whoever performs anything apart from the bishop and the council of presbyters and the deacons is not pure in conscience. (Tr 7.2)
>
> Flee, then, the wicked offshoots that give birth to death-bearing fruit. If anyone should taste it, he dies right then and there, for these are not the Father's plantings. For if they were, they would be appearing as branches of the cross and their fruit would be imperishable. Through it, by his passion, he summons you who are his members. Now a head cannot be born by itself without its body's members, since God promises union, which is himself. (Tr 11.1–2)

Union with Christ, unity in his Body, freely submitting ourselves to spiritual authority and to each other, avoiding heresy, gathering together in worship to receive the Eucharist, making the passion of Christ our own passion, having real living in Christ, attaining to God—these are some of the many themes St. Ignatius stresses over and over again in his life-giving last words. May we read and heed what he offers in his epistles, that we, like him, may get to God.

APOLYTIKION IN THE FOURTH TONE[13]

By sharing in the ways of the apostles, you became a successor to their throne. Through the practice of virtue, you found the way to divine contemplation, O inspired one of God; by teaching the word of truth without error, you defended the faith, even to the shedding of your blood. O Hieromartyr Ignatius, entreat Christ God to save our souls.

KONTAKION IN THE FOURTH TONE[14]

Today you rose from the east, enlightening all of creation with your teachings, and you are crowned with martyrdom, O God-bearing Ignatius.

---

13. http://ww1.antiochian.org/node/32094.
14. http://ww1.antiochian.org/node/32094.

The Epistle of St. Ignatius
to the Ephesians

SALUTATION

Ignatius the God-bearer to the church that is gathered at Ephesus in Asia. You are blessed with greatness by the fullness of God the Father and, as was foreordained before the ages, you are forever headed toward a lasting and unfading glory. Having been united and chosen in real suffering by the will of the Father and Jesus Christ our God, you are a church most worthy of blessing. Abundant greetings to you in Jesus Christ and in blameless joy.

GRATITUDE FOR BISHOP ONESIMUS AND OTHERS

1

1. I welcomed in God your much-beloved name, which you possess by reason of a righteous nature that reflects the faith and love found in Christ Jesus our Savior. Being imitators of God, set aflame by the blood of God, you have perfectly accomplished the task that was so natural to you.

2. For you hurried to see me as soon as you heard that I was departing from Syria in chains for the sake of our common name and hope. You came quickly because you knew that I was hoping by your prayer to succeed in fighting the wild beasts at Rome, so that through attaining martyrdom I might be able to be a disciple.

SALUTATION

Ignatius's other name is *Theophoros*, which means **God-bearer**. His heart is so full of **Christ** our **God** that wherever he goes, **Christ** goes (on **Christ God**, see Rom 9:5 and Titus 2:13). The Roman province of **Asia** was on the Anatolian peninsula (where Turkey now sits) across the Aegean Sea from Greece. Ephesus, its capital, was a major port and center for commercial, civic, and religious affairs. Paul and John wrote to this church (in *The Epistle to the Ephesians* and the letter in Rev 2:1–7). **Foreordained** is often translated *predestined* (Eph 1:5 and 11 within 1:3–14). **Jesus Christ** and **the Father** share one **will** (Tr 1.1). Our **real suffering** is connected to **Jesus's real suffering**, his *very passion*. And our **unity and being chosen** (*elected*) are rooted **in** and demonstrated through **Jesus's** and our own **suffering** (Phil 1.1). Only if "we **suffer** with" **Christ** shall "we reign with him" in **glory** (Rom 8:17–18; 2 Tim 2:12; Sm 4.2; Phil 5.2, 9.2) as "planned" (18.2).

GRATITUDE FOR BISHOP ONESIMUS AND OTHERS

1

1. **Much-beloved name** may refer to their reputation or being *Christian* (1.2, 3.1, 7.1). It is **reflected** in their **righteous nature**. **Christ God** sets them **aflame** as they receive his **blood** in the Eucharist. This energizes and purifies them to **imitate** him (Phil 1.1). Paul refers to **Christ's blood** as **the blood of God** (Acts 20:28). **The task** they **accomplished perfectly** was "hurrying to see" Ignatius (1.2).

2. Ignatius was traveling from Antioch, the capital of **Syria** and the third largest city of the Roman Empire. **Our common name** is *Christian*, **our common hope** is Christ. Ignatius is preparing to become **a disciple** of Christ crucified by triumphing **through martyrdom** in the **Roman** arena. For us to **be** Christ's **disciples**, we must keep **fighting** till death against **the wild beasts** of our passions and **the beastly** demons that incite them.

3. I welcomed your large community in God's name in the person of Onesimus, your bishop, a man of inexpressible love while still in the flesh. Consequently, I request that you love him and take after his likeness in keeping with the way of Jesus Christ. For blessed is he who has graciously gifted you, worthy as you are, with having such a bishop.

2

1. Now about my fellow slave, Burrhus, your deacon by God's appointment, a man blessed in all things: I request that he stay here with me for your honor and your bishop's honor. And as for Crocus, who is worthy of God and of you, I welcomed him as a model example of your love and he refreshed me in every way. May the Father of Jesus Christ also refresh him in the same way, together with Onesimus, Burrhus, Euplus, and Fronto. In them, I have seen how you all show love.

2. May I always draw joy from you, if only I be worthy. It is right, then, in every way to glorify Jesus Christ, who has glorified you all. That way, as you are being perfectly adjusted together through one voluntary obedience by freely submitting yourselves to the bishop and to the council of presbyters, you may be made holy in every way.

3. Ephesus was one of the **largest** cities in Roman Asia. **Bishop** (literally, one who *watches over* or *oversees*) is the title used for the head pastor *over* each church (see 1 Tim 3:1–7, Titus 1:7–9, Mag 2.1, Tr 1.1, Rom 9.1, Pol Sal). **Onesimus** followed Timothy as **bishop** of Ephesus (for more on him, see Phlm 8–21, Col 4:9). Perhaps by being forgiven much, he had become **a man of inexpressible love while still in the flesh** (cf. Luke 7:47). Behind this **bishop** of flesh lies **God**, who is the spiritual **bishop** of all (see Pol Sal). **In Onesimus**, the office of **bishop** is united with God's *charismatic* **gifts** (cf. Pol 2.2). Even when **worthy**, we only have **God's blessings** as a **gift of grace** (a *charism*).

2

1. "Not" by "ordering" (3.1), but by expressing a **request** (a *wish*) is how Ignatius welcomes the leaders sent from Ephesus. His approach is one of humble leadership—to be the servant of all, like his Lord. His concern is for the **honor** of others, not his own. **Crocus**, too, is such a servant, **a model example of love** who shows **refreshing** hospitality to the one he serves. As we **honor** and **refresh** others, **may the Father** likewise **refresh** us. (For more on Ignatius's humility, see 2.2—3.2; and on Polycarp's humility, see Phil 12.1.)

2. The God-bearer is humble when he writes **if only I be worthy**. God goes with him—and with us—because **Jesus Christ** graciously wills to **glorify** his own. Our **right** response to his grace is to **glorify Christ** through **worthy** living. And why would he share his **glory** with us? To make us "**one**, even as" the Father and the Son "are **one**" (John 17:21–22), so that we may "share in" their "**holiness**" (Heb 12:10) and "the world may believe" (John 17:21, Eph 9.3—10.3, Rom 3.2–3). **Made holy** is often translated *sanctified*. **Perfectly adjusted** involves *maturing* (**perfecting**) our love toward God and people, whether believers or not (Phil 12.3, Eph 10.1–2). Our united corporate **obedience** is to be **voluntary** (Pol 2.1, Phil 10.2). **Freely submitting ourselves** to authority in community is essential to Christ's saving purpose: for us all to **be** *mature* in love, which is at the heart of **being made holy** (1 Pet 1:15–16, Matt 5:48, 1 Thess 3:10–13, Phld 11.2). The Greek word for **council of presbyters**, when transliterated, is *presbytery*. (For more on **submission to the bishop and** his **council of presbyters**, see Eph 4.1, Tr 13.2, Phld 8.1, and Sm 8.1.) **Draw joy** can also mean *derive benefit*.

EXHORTATION FOR UNITY WITH THE BISHOP

3

1. I do not order you as if I were somebody. For even though I am in chains for the name, I am not yet perfected in Jesus Christ. In fact, I am just now at the start of learning how to be a disciple, and I speak to you as my fellow students. For I need to be anointed by you with faith, exhortation, endurance, and long-suffering.

2. But since love does not permit me to keep silent about you, I have therefore taken the initiative to exhort you, so that you may run together in step with God's mindset. For, in fact, Jesus Christ, our inseparable life, is the mindset of the Father, just as also the bishops appointed throughout the world are in the mindset of Jesus Christ.

4

1. Consequently, it is right for you to run together in step with the bishop's mindset as, in fact, you are doing, since your council of presbyters, worthy of the name and worthy of God, is attuned to the bishop in the same way as strings are to a lyre. For this reason, Jesus Christ is being hymned in your unanimity and harmonious love.

2. In fact, every one of you must make up this chorus, so that, by being harmonious in one accord and taking your pitch from God in unison, you may sing with one voice through Jesus Christ to the Father. Do this in order that the Father, through your excellent performance, may both hear you and recognize you as members of his Son. It is profitable, then, for you to be in blameless unity, so that you may also and always be partaking of God.

EXHORTATION FOR UNITY WITH THE BISHOP

3

1. **The name** is that of **Jesus Christ,** Christian, or **Christ** God (1.1, 1.2, 7.1; Phil 10.3; Phld 10.1–2). Ignatius humbly calls his readers **fellow students** and says he is **just starting** to **learn how to be a disciple.** Just as athletes were **anointed** with oil, so Ignatius must receive **faith, exhortation, endurance, and long-suffering** from the Ephesians before he can face the wild beasts in the arena at Rome and be **perfected in** martyrdom (Phld 5.1, Pol 2.3).

2. Not out of superiority, but because of **love,** Ignatius cannot **keep silent.** As a fellow sharer in **Christ's inseparable life,** he **exhorts** them to **run together in step with God's mindset** (or *intention,* here and elsewhere). This **mindset** is not nebulous, but concrete: **Jesus Christ is the mindset of the Father.** And **the mindset of Jesus Christ** is itself **inseparable** from his **bishops,** because he shares his **life** with them.

4

1. The people can **run together in step with the bishop's mindset** because he is leading them in the race that leads to a full participation in the "life" **Christ** "shares" with us (3.2, Phld 2.2, Pol 1.3, Mag 11.1, Tr 11.2). They can trust their other ministers because they are **worthy of God** and in **tune** with **the bishop.** In-tune leadership brings forth a people of **unanimity** who **hymn Jesus Christ** with a **love** that is **harmonious** (or more literally, *has* one *sound like a symphony*).

2. Our "hymn" raised to **Jesus Christ** (4.1) is now offered **through** him to **the Father. Hearing** the **excellence** of our **performance in unison** (or *unity*), **the Father recognizes** that he is *listening to* the **members of his Son's** Body. In the Orthodox Church, this occurs in the Divine Liturgy when the Eucharist is celebrated (solemnly performed). Liturgy means *work of the people.* By this **blameless** and **united** work we manifest our common life together and **partake of** (*participate in*) the life of **the Father** and **his Son** (2 Pet 1:4). Our staying **united** to each other **also** enables our **partaking of God** outside the Liturgy. Our **unity** with **the Father** and **his Son** includes our **unity** with all of **the Fathers** of the Church from its very beginning.

5

1. For if I myself in a short time came to have such an intimate acquaintance with your bishop—a kind not human, but spiritual, how much more do I bless you who are mingled with him in the same way as the church is with Jesus Christ and Jesus Christ is with the Father, so that all may be harmonious in unity.

2. Let no one be deceived: unless someone be within the altar, he lacks the bread of God. For if the prayer of one or two has such might, how much more that of the bishop and the whole church.

3. Therefore, whoever does not come together in the common assembly thereby demonstrates his arrogance and has separated himself. For it is written, "God opposes the arrogant." Therefore, let us be careful not to oppose the bishop, that we may freely be in submission to God.

6

1. And the more anyone sees the bishop keeping silent, the more he should fear him. For we ought to receive every steward whom the Master sends to dispense the goods of the house on his behalf in the same way that we would the one who sent him. Clearly, then, we must hold the bishop in the same regard as the Lord himself.

5

1. Just as the faithful **mingle** their voices in song (4.2), so are they to **mingle** their lives with their bishop in a manner more **intimate** than the **short acquaintance** that Ignatius has had with Onesimus. This **mingling** is **spiritual** and from the **Spirit** (see Sm 3.2). **All** may refer to *everyone, everything,* or *every voice.*

2. **No one** and **he** may refer to the celebrant (Tr 7.2) or to any**one** else. During the Liturgy, **the bread** that **the** Orthodox **bishop** or his authorized presbyter puts on **the altar** table becomes **the bread of God** himself. **Altar** may refer to the area around **the altar** table that Orthodox call **the altar**. To be outside **the altar** means to be outside the communion of **the church** and beyond the nourishment of **God's bread**, for the Eucharist is served only **in the church**. (On **one or two**, compare Jesus's words on **two or** three in Matt 18:19–20.)

3. We gather **together in the common assembly** to break "bread" in the Eucharist (5.2, 13.1, 20.2; Mag 7.1–2; Phld 6.2, 10.1; Mart Pol 18.3). Those who **separate** (that is, *self-excommunicate*) themselves include the Gnostics. **"God opposes the arrogant"** (Prov 3:34 LXX/3:37 OSB; quoted in Jas 4:6, 1 Pet 5:5) because they lack a **submissive** spirit and spurn his banquet.

6

1. **The bishop** may **keep silent** because he is withholding his blessing from "the arrogant" (5.3), communing with God in his heart (4.2), or just acting wisely as a man of few words (Jas 1:19; Prov 11:12/11:10 OSB, 17:27/17:29 OSB; Sir 20:5–8, 32.7–8). Ignatius himself valued **silence** and brevity (Eph 15.1–2, Mag 14.1, Rom 8.2, Phld 1.1, Pol 7.3). The bishop's **silence should** evoke **fear**, for **the Master** of **the house** expects us to **receive the bishop as** though he were **the Lord himself**.

EPHESIAN ORTHODOXY IN FLESH AND SPIRIT

2. But as for you, Onesimus himself highly praises your well-ordered and godly conduct, reporting that you all live in accordance with truth and that there is no heresy dwelling among you. Instead, you do not so much as listen to anybody unless he speaks truthfully about Jesus Christ.

7

1. For there are some who have the habit of carrying the name around with wicked guile, while acting in ways unworthy of God. You should shun them like wild beasts, for they are mad dogs that bite without warning. You must be on your guard against them, since their bite is all but incurable.

2. There is one physician,
fleshy and spiritual,
born and unborn,
in man God,
in death true life,
both from Mary and from God,
first subject to suffering and then above suffering,
Jesus Christ, our Lord.

8

1. Therefore, let no one delude you, as indeed you are not deluded, since you belong entirely to God. For whenever bickering, which has the capacity to torment, is in no way entrenched among you, then indeed are you living God's way. I am your humble offering and I am purifying myself for you Ephesians, a church famous to the ages.

EPHESIAN ORTHODOXY IN FLESH AND SPIRIT

2. Because the Ephesians **live truthfully**, allow **no heresy** to take root, and only **listen to** what is **true about Jesus Christ, Onesimus** does not "keep silent" (6.1) with them. **Heresy** is the opposite of "harmonious love" (4.1) and involves a sect and leader that put themselves first and cut themselves off from that "inseparable **life**" (3.2) which is in **Jesus Christ** and his Catholic Church (see Sm 8.2). Having sundered themselves from "the **true** vine" (John 15:1–10), they must **speak** falsely **about Jesus Christ**.

7

1. Unlike Ignatius, the **God-*bearer*,** who **carries God** by grace, the Gnostics ungraciously **carry around the name** of "Jesus Christ" (6.2, 3.1) like **mad dogs carry** rabies. They **carry the name** as a ruse by which to infect others. No wonder **their bite is all but incurable.** (For more on the Gnostics, see 8.2.)

2. This early creedal statement may be a hymn (for other possible creed-like hymns, see 1 Tim 3:16, Pol 3.2, Sm 1.1b–2, Eph 19.2–3). The **one physician** who can "cure" (see 7.1) is *human*, sharing our **flesh**. But now his **flesh** has become **spiritual**ized by the resurrection (Sm 3.2, Eph 8.2). **From Mary,** Christ was **born** a *human being*. Yet **from God** and as **God**, he is **unborn**, always existing with the Father. Fully *human*, partaking of our **flesh** unto **death**, he is now revealed to be **God** by the triumph of **true life** in the resurrection. Having **suffered** unto **death** like us, he now reigns over **death** and mortal **suffering** (Pol 3.2, Eph 1:20–21).

8

1. **God entirely** possesses us when we **live** our lives his **way** (Gal 5:22–26). Such a union has **no room** for **delusion** or **capacity** for **bickering** over what **belongs to** us. Literally, **entrenched** is *poking through*. Ignatius **is purifying** himself for martyrdom, so that he may become a **humble offering** (a *peripsema*) **for** the **Ephesians** in the arena of Rome (18.1, Tr 13.3). At one time **Ephesus** was known for its temple of Artemis (Acts 19:35). Now it will be known for its **church** that is **famous to the ages** (or *Aeons*; see Eph 19.2).

2. Those who are fleshly cannot make a practice of doing spiritual things, and those who are spiritual cannot make a practice of doing fleshly things. In the same way, faith is incapable of the deeds of unbelief, and unbelief is incapable of the deeds of faith. But even those things that you do in relation to the flesh, they are spiritual, for you do all things in Jesus Christ.

9

1. I have learned, however, that certain people with evil teaching have passed by us on their way from your city. You did not allow them to sow among you, but stopped up your ears to avoid letting in what was sown by them. This was because you are temple stones, prepared beforehand for use in building God the Father's edifice. You are being hoisted up to the heights by the crane of Jesus Christ, which is the cross, using the Holy Spirit for a cable. And your faith is what leads you higher, and love the way that carries you up to God.

2. And so you are all fellow travelers on the way, God-bearers and temple-bearers, Christ-bearers, bearers of holy things, who are in every way arrayed in the commandments of Jesus Christ. With you I too rejoice, since I have been counted worthy to converse with you through what I am writing and to congratulate you that—in line with a different kind of life—you love nothing but God alone.

2. "Everyone who abides in him does not **practice** sin" and "**cannot practice** sin" (1 John 3:6, 9; Eph 10.3). Christians will struggle with sin, but if they strive to "abide" **in Jesus Christ**, they will not make a lifestyle of it (Rom 8:5). **Deeds of unbelief** are *faithless* **deeds** (on *faithless*, see Tr 10.1, Sm 2.1). Ignatius starts out contrasting **fleshly** (*carnal*) with **spiritual**, with a concern for the sins of **the flesh**, but ends up using **flesh** as a synonym for our **fleshy** bodies. **In Jesus Christ, flesh** is made **spiritual**; without him, **flesh** remains **flesh** and ever inclines to **fleshly** (*carnal*) sin (Eph 7.2, Ag Heresies 5.6.1). Ignatius's teaching in this and the next section is aimed at the Gnostics (see 7.1–2, 16.1–2, 19.2; Tr 5.1—7.2).

9

1. **Evil teachers** have **passed by** Smyrna (where Ignatius is) **on their way from** Ephesus (where his audience is). **Sow among you** may be translated **sow** *into* **you. Ears of stone** to heresy help avoid **hearts of stone to God.** What a great honor for **the Father** through **Jesus Christ** and **the Holy Spirit** to **prepare** us to be the **temple of God,** where he will dwell in us forever (John 14:23). What a motivation **to avoid letting in evil teaching!** Central to this **preparation** is **the cross:** as we present ourselves as lifeless **stones, the Holy Spirit** will pick us **up** and raise us to where our **faith** can **lead** us **higher** to **the way** of sacrificial **love** that ends in **God** (see 1 Pet 2:4–10). St. Patrick's words speak to this: "I was like a **stone** lying deep in the mire, and in his mercy he lifted me **up** and placed me on the top of the wall" (Confess 12). Later on he "spent" his life on the Irish (Confess 37, 53; 2 Cor 12:15; Tr 2.2).

2. As pilgrims in procession, we move forward together in "**the way**" of "love" (9.1), **bearing God,** his **temple** (which we are), **Christ,** and **holy things** (that is, virtues). We should all become **God-bearers** like St. Ignatius was—and is. Through our obedience to **the commandments of Jesus Christ** we **array** ourselves in magnificent festal garments. This obedience is personal, based on our relationship with **Jesus Christ** and out of **love** for **God alone. Love** makes the Christian **kind of life** (*bios*) **different** from this world's merely *biological* **life** of lust and pride (1 John 2:15–16; Eph 10.1–3, 8.2; Rom 7.2–3; Mart Pol 3.1; Phld 11.1).

10

1. As for the people that are different than you, keep on praying on their behalf without ceasing—for in their case there is hope for repentance—that they may get to God. Let the result at least be that they are instructed like disciples by your actions.

2. In answer to their outbursts of anger, you be meek; in response to their many boasts, you be humble. You meet their slanders with repeated prayers, their error with firm, faithfully-held convictions, and their untamed wildness with civil responses. And do not quickly imitate their example.

3. Let us prove to be their brothers and sisters by forbearance, and let us eagerly strive to be imitators of the Lord. (Who has been more wronged? Who more cheated? Who more rejected?) Do this so that no weed planted by the devil may be found among you, but rather that in complete purity and self-control you may abide in Christ Jesus in flesh and in spirit.

10

1. Ignatius exhorts them to **keep on praying** (1 Thess 5:17) for *those unlike* them in the world since **they** may yet **repent**. The **actions** of Christians may still **instruct** and make **disciples** when their words cannot. Ignatius uses **get to God** when speaking in general (Mag 1.2, Sm 9.2), reserving the more intensive "attaining to God" for martyrs, specifically himself (Eph 12.2) and Polycarp (Pol 2.3).

2. Ignatius now proceeds to set forth how our "different kind of life" (9.2) can make "disciples" (10.1) of those in the world—those who are **angry, boastful, slanderous, in error, and untamed**. The root for **untamed wildness** is the same as for **wild** beast. Though we may not be fed to **wild** beasts, such people will confront us where we live (Rom 5.1, 2 Pet 2:12–13). Whenever this happens, may we **meet** them **with prayers** and **civil responses**, rather than **quick** reactions. And may we show them **meekness, humility,** and **firm convictions. Meekness** is *gentle, unassuming, bridled strength*.

3. If **by forbearance** we **prove to be their brothers and sisters**, they may become his "disciples" (10.1). The word for **brothers**, here translated **brothers and sisters**, refers to all the members of a church family unless otherwise indicated (as in Sm 13.1, Pol 5.1, Phil 3.1). Each one of us must respond to those outside the Church the way our **Lord** did, and nobody **has been more wronged, cheated,** or **rejected** than he was. **Abiding in Christ Jesus** involves all that we are (our **flesh and spirit**). If we **eagerly,** yea *diligently,* **strive** to *remain* **in him** in *total* **purity and self-control,** then we can avoid any **plant** of **the devil** that might choke out our community's life (Tr 6.1–2, 11.1–2; Phld 3.1; Mg 6.1).

SPIRITUAL WARFARE

11

1. These are the last times. For the time that remains, let us be ashamed. Let us fear the long-suffering of God, lest it become our condemnation. For either we should fear the wrath to come or love the present grace, one of the two—only let us be found in Christ Jesus experiencing real living.

2. Let nothing suit you apart from him. It is in him that I carry about these chains as spiritual pearls. By them may it be granted me to arise through your prayer. And of this prayer may it be granted me to ever be a partaker. That way I may be found to share in the lot of the Ephesian Christians, who have, in fact, always been in agreement with the apostles by the power of Jesus Christ.

SPIRITUAL WARFARE

11

1. **God suffers longs** with us (2 Pet 3:9, 15; 1 Pet 3:20). For the **remaining time** of our life, **let us shame** *ourselves* before him in "repentance" (Mag 12.1, Rom 2:4). Confessing (unhiding) our lack of "purity and self-control" (10.3) can bring bountiful forgiveness, restoration, and healing, "for there is a **shame** that leads to glory and **grace**" (Sir 4:21, 26). Whether we **shame** *ourselves* out of **fear** or out of **love**, we must endure to the end **in Christ Jesus**. This end includes the *conclusion* of our lives, as well as all the steps involved in accomplishing this *goal* (Eph 14.1–2, Mag 5.1—6.1, Phil 5.2). We often need both **fear** and **love**; in fact, "the **fear of God** is the beginning of **loving** him" (Sir 25:12 in the Church of Greece's LXX). Even so, over **time**, may "perfect **love** cast out" our "**fear**" (1 John 4:18).

2. The word for **apart from** can also be translated *without*, both here and elsewhere. **Nothing** should be **suitable** *without* **Christ**. But when we are **found in him**, even the binding **chains** of our circumstances, limitations, and lackings that would hold us down become a singular necklace of **spiritual pearls** (Mag 1.2; Tr 5.2, 12.2; Phil 1.1) that urges us on to **rise** *up* and reach God. **The Ephesian Christians** are part of a **powerful apostolic** church (Rev 2:2). **Through** their joint **prayer**, offered when they celebrate the Eucharist together, Ignatius hopes to be faithful unto martyrdom. **And** he also hopes **to ever be** included in their **prayer** until he **shares in** their **lot** (destiny) by **rising** in the resurrection with them. Here we see corporate **prayer** for the departed in the first hundred years of the Church (2 Tim 1:16–18, Phil 12.2–3, Mart Pol 8.1).

12

1. I know who I am and to whom I write. I am a convict; you are the ones who have been shown mercy. I am in peril, while you are safe and secure.

2. You are the highway for those being slain for God and fellow initiates with Paul, the sanctified one, a man in possession of a good testimony by his martyrdom and worthy of blessing—may it be granted me to be found following under his footsteps whenever I may attain to God—who in every epistle remembers you in Christ Jesus.

12

1. Ignatius is **writing** as a *condemned criminal* who is **in** outward **peril** of execution in Rome and possible **peril** of failing the test of martyrdom. Another **peril** facing the saint, one of grave concern to him, is the prospect of not being executed (Rom 4.1, 3; 5.3). In this section (and the ones that precede and follow it: 11.2 and 12.2), he humbly sets forth why he needs their prayer and has confidence in it. His real humility is evident throughout this and his other epistles and stands in marked contrast to the criticisms of some of his academic detractors who often portray him as a kind of power-hungry and unbalanced bishop who is intent on having his own way in Antioch and throughout all the churches to which he writes (for more on his humility, see comments on Phil Sal).

2. Ephesus lay on the *route* to Rome for criminals from the provinces bound for combat in the arena. This **highway** had been traveled by **St. Paul**. Now Ignatius wants to **follow** in **his martyric footsteps**—actually **under** them, since he sees himself that far below **Paul** (see Mart Pol 22.1 on us following "in" Polycarp's "**footsteps**"). Through the mysteries (sacraments) of baptism and the Eucharist, the Ephesian Christians were **fellow initiates** with **Paul** in the death of **Christ**. In fact, some of them might have been **initiated** by **Paul** himself. Ignatius hopes to follow **Paul's** example of **martyrdom** by means of the "prayer of the Ephesians" (11.2). He uses the expression **attain to** to describe his *successful attainment of reaching* **God** or **Jesus Christ**, and thus his *obtaining* **God**, through his active acceptance of his lot of **martyrdom** (on **attain**, see Eph 1.2; Tr 12.2–3, 13.3; Rom 1.1–2, 5.3; Sm 11.1; Pol 2.3; on *reach* God, see Rom 6.1, 3; Phil Sal commentary; on get to God, see Eph 10.1). **In every epistle** unites the Ephesians to all the faithful **remembered** by **Paul** in all his other **epistles**.

13

1. Eagerly exert effort, then, for your meetings to be closer together as you celebrate God's Eucharist and bring glory to him. For whenever you gather close together in the common assembly, the powers of Satan are cast down; and his destructiveness is undone by your unanimity in the faith.

2. Nothing is better than peace. By it all warfare of heavenly and earthly powers is brought to an end.

FAITH AND LOVE

14

1. None of these things escapes your notice whenever you have perfect faith and love for Jesus Christ. These are the beginning and the end of life. The beginning is faith, the end is love; and when the two come together in unity, you have God. Everything else leading to a noble character follows in due course.

2. Nobody professing faith practices sin, nor does anyone possessing love practice hate. "The tree is known from its fruit." So those professing to belong to Christ shall be seen by what they practice. For what matters is not what one promises now, but whether by the power of faith one be found continuing to the end.

13

1. **The Eucharist** (*Thank Offering*) is a communal banquet where we offer ourselves to God in *thanks* for his creation, providence, and redemption. In turn, he offers himself to us to feast upon (John 6:30–58; Gen 3:1–6, 22). Ignatius urges **eager effort** for a **closer**, *more intimate* communion: our shared lives, his shared body and blood (see Did 14.1–2 on confession and Eucharist). These practices **cast down the powers of Satan** and maintain our **unanimity in the faith**, by which **Satan's destructiveness is undone**. Such worship **brings glory to God. Close** can mean *frequent* (**close** in time) and *tight-knit* (**close** in relationship). Ignatius appears to mean both (Pol 4.2, Heb 10:25).

2. This short section is set in the context of the Eucharistic Liturgy (13.1). Christ's **peace** offering of himself upon the **heavenly** altar shows that the reign of the evil **heavenly powers** has **ended** (Eph 2:13–17; Heb 9:24–26, 2:14–15). Christ's **peace** experienced in the Liturgy brings **peace** around us, between us, and within us—and **peace** triumphant. By the **peace** that his victory brings we can keep Paul's admonition to "be at **peace** with everyone" (Rom 12:18, Matt 5:23–24).

FAITH AND LOVE

14

1. **These things** refers to spiritual "warfare" that triumphs through **unity** (13.1–2). Here Ignatius stresses **faith** as **beginning** principle **and love** as **the end** (*goal* and *conclusion*) for **unity** (see comments on 11.1). **Whenever faith and love come together, we have God**, both in corporate **unity** and **unity** of heart (Ps 86:11 MT, Tr 13.2, Phld 6.2). The next section depicts what **a noble character** looks like.

2. What we **practice** shows our **faith** and **love** (cf. 8.2). **Belonging to Christ** involves behaving like him. We are to make a **practice** of it every day until **the end**. "**The tree is known from its fruit**," our Lord said (Matt 12:33). "**Faith without works is dead**," said his brother (Jas 2:20). The **matter** Ignatius has in mind is his martyrdom at **the end**, and **the power of faith** he speaks of is his unflagging fortitude that must **continue to the end** in the face of the wild beasts (see 1.2). "**Faith** is the proof of things not seen" (Heb 11:1).

15

1. Better it is to keep silent and be real than to go on speaking and not be. Teaching is a beautiful thing, if the one talking act accordingly. So there is one Teacher who spoke and it occurred, and even what he accomplished in silence is worthy of the Father.

2. The one who truly possesses the word of Jesus can even hear his still silence, so that he may be perfect, putting into practice what he says and being known through what he does silently.

3. Nothing escapes the Lord's notice; instead, even our secrets are near him. Therefore, let us do everything as though he were dwelling in us, that we may be his temples and he himself may be in us as our God. Such, in fact, he definitely is, and this shall become apparent to us by our loving him rightly.

16

1. Do not be deluded, my brothers and sisters: those who corrupt households "shall not inherit the kingdom of God."

15

1. **Keeping silent is** good (see 6.1). Inserting **real** after **be** follows Greek usage. We should avoid **speaking** about what we have **not** learned from our own experience (Mag 4.1, Rom 3.2). **Teachers** ought to be like the **one Teacher who** did what he taught. Not only did creation **happen** when he **spoke** (Gen 1:3, Ps 32/33:9), but redemption was *taking place* as our Paschal lamb **kept silent** while he was being sheared (Isa 53:7).

2. **His** could mean *its* and refer to **the word's silence**. The antecedent for **he** is **the one who possesses the word**, not **Jesus**. The Greek for **still silence** is *hesychia* (also found in Eph 19.1). Orthodox hesychastic spirituality emphasizes being **still** and **silent** (that is, *hushed*) before God As an aid on the path of **perfection** (*maturity*), *hesychi*a can move the believer beyond **words** to the **Word** himself. An important practice in this journey is the repetition of the **Jesus** Prayer: "Lord **Jesus** Christ, Son of God, have mercy on me, a sinner." This prayer helps us **silence** all the vain **words** that take our thoughts captive (17.1, 2 Cor 10:3–5, 1 Thess 5:17).

3. When we keep silent about **our secret** sins, the Most High still **notices** them (Sir 39:1, 19–20). Because he is **our God in us, everything** is **near him**. Living like **he dwells in us** will enable us to **love him** the **right** way. Then, "whenever **he** may **appear**" to us—whether now, at our end, or at the end of the age—"we may have confidence and not shrink back from **him** in shame at his coming" (1 John 2:28, Pol 7.2, Eph 11.1, Mal 3:2). **This shall become apparent to us by our loving him rightly** can be rendered *he shall appear before our face because we love* **him rightly**.

16

1. Ignatius is quoting Paul on who will **"not inherit the kingdom"** (1 Cor 6:9–10, Eph 5:5–6, Phil 5.3, Phld 3.3). **Households** refers to families, to the **household** of "faith" (16.2), and possibly to **house** churches. The Gnostics and other heretics are **those who corrupt**.

2. If, then, those engaging in the sins of the flesh incurred death, how much more shall someone else incur if by evil teaching he should corrupt the faith of God? It was for this faith that Jesus Christ was crucified. Such a person, because he has defiled himself, shall depart into the unquenchable fire. Likewise, too, the one listening to him.

GOD'S PLAN OF SALVATION IN JESUS CHRIST

17

1. The Lord accepted anointing with myrrh upon his head for this reason, that he might breathe incorruptibility into the Church. Do not be anointed with the reeking, filthy teaching of the ruler of this age, lest he take you captive and deprive you of the life that is set before you.

2. Why do we not all become wise when we receive the knowledge of God, which is Jesus Christ? Why do we foolishly perish, ignoring the gracious gift that the Lord has truly sent?

18

1. My very spirit is a humble offering to the cross, which is a scandal to unbelievers, but to us salvation and eternal life. Where is the wise? Where is the debater? Where is the boasting of the so-called intelligent?

2. The consequence recorded for the adulterous and idolatrous Israelites of old was temporal **death** (Num 25:1–9, 1 Cor 10:8), but those who now "**corrupt**" the faith of God's "**household**" (16.1)—whether by **sins of the flesh or spirit**—**shall incur** the eternal penalty of **unquenchable fire. God's faith** (the Christian **faith**) **teaches** about **God**, creation, and man's salvation, **for** which **Jesus Christ was crucified. Evil teaching** is an **evil** matter to God. **Listening to him** means *hearing* **such a person** *and doing what he says.*

GOD'S PLAN OF SALVATION IN JESUS CHRIST

17

1. **The Lord accepted anointing with** sweet-smelling **myrrh** (Matt 26:6–13) as a sign of **his** coming victory over **corruption** in the grave. Once resurrected, he **breathed his incorruptible** Spirit **into the Church**, starting with the apostles (John 20:19–23, Sm 3.2, Gen 2:7, 1 Cor 15:45). Rather than **reeking** like **the filth** of decaying heretical **teaching**, we ought to be "a sweet-smelling fragrance of Christ to God" (2 Cor 2:15, Eph 5:2, Phil 4:18, Mart Pol 15.2). By this, we can avoid the **captivating** decadence **of this age**—and its **ruler**, the devil—and cling to **the Lord's incorruptible life.**

2. Just **receiving Christ** will not make us **wise**. We must grasp God's way to **wisdom**: "the cross" (see 18.1). The **gracious gift** (*charism*) is the "anointing" of the Spirit (17.1, Pol 2.2), whom **the Lord** promised to **send us** (John 14:26, 15:26, 16:7; Acts 2:33). He will lead us to the cross (Rom 8:13–17, Eph 9.1).

18

1. **Humble offering** originally meant *offscouring* (see 8.1, 1 Cor 4:13). Do not be surprised when **unbelievers** treat **us** like **the cross's scum**. This section draws heavily on the paradoxes of 1 Corinthians 1:18–30, which contrasts God's foolishness with man's **wisdom**. Through **the cross** we become a sweet-smelling fragrance (17.1), as did the **humble** and **spiritual** pastor, St. Ignatius.

2. For our God, Jesus the Christ, was carried in the womb by Mary in keeping with God's plan of salvation—being both from the seed of David and the Holy Spirit—and was born and baptized that by his passion he might purify the water.

19

1. Both the virginity of Mary and her giving birth escaped the notice of the ruler of this age, and so also the death of the Lord—three mysteries of a cry wrought in the still silence of God.

2. How, then, was he made manifest to the Aeons?
  A star shone forth in heaven
  brighter than all the stars—
  and its light was beyond describing,
  and its novelty produced astonishment.
  Now all the other stars,
  together with sun and moon,
  formed a chorus round the star—
  while its very light was far outshining them all.
  And there was perplexity
  over the source of this novelty,
  which was so unlike them.

2. The incarnation is central to **God's plan of salvation** (as seen here, in 19.1—20.1, and throughout Irenaeus's *Against Heresies*). **Jesus** comes both as **our God** and as **the Christ**, *the Messiah*, our promised human deliverer. As a man, he was descended **from David** through **Mary**. At his baptism, **Christ our God** begins to conquer the devil and the powers of darkness. **His passion** involves his voluntary *suffering* at his baptism, in the wilderness, and finally on the cross (Matt 3:13–15, 4:1–11; Phil 2:5–11). He **purifies the water** of **baptism** of every im**pure** cosmic spirit (see Gen 1:2) in order to unite us to **God**. The Orthodox service for holy **baptism** says that **Christ** did "'hallow the streams of Jordan, sending down upon them. . . [the] **Holy Spirit**, and did crush the heads of the dragons who lurked there'" (http://ww1.antiochian. org/sites/default/files/liturgical_guides/holy-sat-vesperal-lit_final.pdf).

19

1. **The mysteries God** "planned" (18.2) *were hidden from* **the ruler of this age**, so he did not understand when **the Virgin** conceived and **gave birth** and **the Lord** suffered **death** (Isa 7:14; Matt 1:23–25; Luke 1:27, 34–35, 2:7; 1 Cor 2:7–8). This was because **God** was keeping **still** and **silent**. (On **stillness** and **silence**, see 15.1–2, Mag 8.2, and Rom 14:24–25 (or 16:25–26), where Paul gloried in "the revelation of the **mystery** kept in **silence** for long ages.") But now the **three mysteries** he set in motion **cry** out to be proclaimed. When these **mysteries** began to unfold, there were also audible **cries: Mary's cry** of exultation at the Annunciation (Luke 1:46–55) and our **Lord's** "**cry**" of victory at his **death**: "It is finished!" (Mark 15:37, John 19:30).

2. Ignatius may have chosen the word **aeons** (usually translated *ages*), rather than *cosmos* (world) to mock the emerging mythology of the Gnostics, who claimed to have special knowledge for salvation (Tr 5.1–2). **Aeons** became a term they used for their mishmash of divine emanations (see *Against Heresies*, especially Book 1). To Ignatius, these were none other than the **heavenly** powers of darkness in league with "the ruler of this age [*aeon*]" (19.1). Our Lord's **manifestation** (*appearance*) to the **Aeons** was **like** that of an incomparable **novel star**, reminiscent of the one that pointed the magi to the Lord. This **perplexed** both the Gnostics and their **Aeons**, who only saw the **star**, but could not see the Lord, who was **so unlike them**. (Ignatius's **star** narrative draws on several sources: Gen 37:5–11; Wis 7:21, 26, 29–30; 11–19; and Matt 2:1–15.)

3. By it, all magic started to dissolve,
   and every bond to vanish;
   ignorance born of evil began to suffer conquest,
   and the ancient kingdom started crumbling,
   when God appeared as man
   bringing the newness of eternal life.
   So what had been concluded by God
   was receiving its beginning;
   henceforth all things were in tumult,
   because the destruction of death was under way.

20

1. If Jesus Christ should count me worthy in response to your prayer, and if it be his will, I shall, in a second piece I am going to write you, further develop for you the explanation I have started about the plan of salvation concerning the new man Jesus Christ, dealing with his faithfulness and his love, his passion and resurrection.

3. From the time **when God appeared as man bringing the newness** (or the *"novelty"*, as in 19.2; Phld 9.2) **of eternal life**, the entire cosmos was **in tumult, because the destruction of death** had begun. **The destruction of death** is one of the ways that Ignatius pictures redemption: **man** free from the grip **of death**, sin, and the devil (13.1, 20.2; Rom 5:8–21; Col 2:9–15; Heb 2:14–15). The triumphal tone of this hymnic piece is echoed in St. John Chrysostom's famous Paschal homily. This victorious, **living newness** is **God's** *novel* **conclusion** to *humanity's* story.

20

1. We have no **second work** from Ignatius to the Ephesians. Nor do we have another instance of his using the Greek word *oikonomia*, rendered here and in 18.2 as **"plan of salvation."** *Oikonomia* is traditionally translated *economy* or *dispensation* and includes God's **plan** (or *arrangement*) and its *management* (as in Eph 6.1, Rom 1.2; for the most important New Testament verse and passage on *oikonomia*, see Eph 1:10 within Eph 1:9–14). The divine *economy* **of salvation** is rooted in **the new man Jesus Christ** (Mag 1.2, Rom 6.1–2). It bears fruit in us as we manifest **his faithfulness and love** through the power of **his passion and resurrection.** An alternate translation for the four items beginning with **his faithfulness** and ending with **resurrection** has a different emphasis: *faith in him and love for him due to his passion and resurrection.* But Ignatius may well have had both meanings in mind, so that we might consider both as we ponder the mystery of our redemption in **Christ.**

2. Especially shall I do this if the Lord should happen to reveal to me that all of you, individually and collectively, continue to gather together in grace, by name, in one faith, and in one Jesus Christ, who came from the lineage of David according to the flesh, who is the Son of Man and Son of God. That way you may obey the bishop and the council of presbyters with an undisturbed mind as you break one bread, which is the medicine of immortality, the antidote that prevents dying and enables living in Jesus Christ forever.

REQUEST FOR PRAYER AND FAREWELL

21

1. As for me, my life is an offering devoted to you and to those whom you sent for God's honor to Smyrna. From there I am writing you, giving thanks to the Lord and loving Polycarp the same way I also love you. Remember me, as Jesus Christ also remembers you.

2. Ignatius hopes to write them again and further explain the divine "plan of salvation" involving **Jesus Christ, the Son of Man and Son of God** (20.1, 18.2; Rom 1:3–4). **Came from the lineage of David according to the flesh** means he *was a physical descendant* **of David** (18.2, Tr 9.1, Sm 1.1, Luke 2:4). Ignatius **shall** write again **if the Lord** confirms by a special charism of **revelation that** they are all **continuing** in communion with each other and in **obedience** to their leaders. By **continuing to gather together** to receive the Eucharist **in grace, by name, in one faith, and in one Jesus Christ** (see Dem 61), they can **obey** their leaders with **an undisturbed** (and *undistracted*) **mind** and partake of his **one** sacramental body with his **one** Body of believers. This **prevents dying and enables living** *continuously* **in Jesus Christ** (Mag 1.2, Sm 12.2).

REQUEST FOR PRAYER AND FAREWELL

21

1. St. Ignatius's whole **life is** an *antipsychon*, a sacrificial **offering devoted to** others. This term involves *giving one's life* for others as a kind of *ransom*, whether or not resulting in one's death, as happened with Ignatius and our Lord **Jesus Christ**. (Greek words similar in meaning to *antipsychon* are employed in Matt 20:28 and Mark 10:45.) Ignatius uses *antipsychon* three other times (Sm 10.2, Pol 2.3, Pol 6.1). *4 Maccabees*, a work that may have come from first-century Antioch, used it of Jewish martyrdom (6:29, 17:22; also see Frend, *Martyrdom and Persecution*, 152–53). *Antipsychon* has affinities with *peripsema* (humble **offering**; 8.1, 18.1) and *hilasterion* (expiation; Rom 3:25).

2. Pray for the Church that is in Syria, from which I am being led away in chains to Rome. Although the least of the faithful there, I have been counted worthy to be found serving God's honor. May you fare well in God the Father and in Jesus Christ, our common hope.

2. Ignatius does not say **in** *Antioch*, but **in Syria**. While **Syria** obviously includes *Antioch*, they are not synonymous terms. **The Church that is in Syria** (a phrase also used in Mag 14.12, Tr 13.1, Rom 9.1), refers to all the churches in **Syria** collectively, not just to Ignatius's own **church in** *Antioch* (for more on this collective use of **Church**, see Rom Sal, 2.2; Tr 13.1; on Ignatius's later mention of *Antioch* and **Syria** together, see Phld 10.1; Sm 11.1–2; Pol 7.1–3, 8.2). He refers to himself as **the least** member on several occasions (Tr 13.1, Rom 9.2, Sm 11.1; St. Patrick, in Confess 56, speaks of himself as "one of **the least**" of God's ministers). Ignatius considers himself **honored to be found in chains** on his way **to** martyrdom in **Rome** (for how his understanding of **honor** contrasts sharply with the **Roman** view, see Pol 5.2). "For the **honor** that suffices," St. Patrick says, "is the one not yet seen, but believed on in the heart" (Confess 54). If, like Ignatius, we would embrace the cross of our personal struggles as an **honor** to bear, we could experience the resurrection in our lives in the here and now (Mag 11.1), as well as in the hereafter (Eph 14.2), all the while taking courage **in our common hope, Jesus Christ**. Then would we **fare well** as we continued to abide **in Christ** and **the Father** (8.2, 10.3; Pol 8.3).

The Epistle of St. Ignatius
to the Magnesians

CONTENTS

SALUTATION

Ignatius the God-bearer to the church that is gathered at Magnesia on the Maeander. You have been blessed by the grace of God the Father in Christ Jesus our Savior. In him I embrace you, and I bid you abundant greetings in God the Father and in Jesus Christ.

GRATITUDE FOR BISHOP DAMAS AND OTHERS

1

1. When I learned of the highly-disciplined nature of your love toward God, I gladly decided to address you in the faith of Jesus Christ.

2. Inasmuch, then, as I have been counted worthy of a name most pleasing to God, I sing the praises of the churches in the chains that I carry about. And I request that there be a union in them of flesh and spirit coming from Jesus Christ, our continuous life; and a union of both faith and love, to which nothing is preferable; and, above all, a union of Jesus and the Father. By this—if we patiently endure every abuse of the ruler of this age and manage to escape—we shall get to God.

SALUTATION

Magnesia was an important commercial center **on the Maeander** River in Roman Asia fourteen miles east of Ephesus. **Ignatius**, like John, links our relationship with **God the Father** to our saving relationship with **Jesus Christ** (1 John 1:3, 2:1, 2:22–24; 2 John 3, 9). In Ignatius's Salutations and farewells, **embrace** often takes the place of other words for *salute* or *greet*.

GRATITUDE FOR BISHOP DAMAS AND OTHERS

1

1. Christian **love** ought to be **highly disciplined**. Ascetical self-**discipline** can create a humble vessel for holding and sharing **God's love** (Mart Pol 18.3). This is the whole point of the monastic vocation. In this epistle, Ignatius **addresses the faith of Jesus Christ** as it contrasts with **the faith of the Judaizers**.

2. The **name most pleasing to God** is *Christian* or *God-bearer*. Either way Ignatius will live up to his **name** if by **faithfully** *bearing* his **chains** he **endures every abuse** and so **manages to escape** and **get to God** (Luke 21:36). His first **request** is for their corporate and personal **union** with the **flesh and spirit** *of* Jesus Christ, "the perfect man" (Sm 4.2). As we partake of his glorified **flesh** (body) in the Eucharist, we become his Body and our **flesh and spirit** are reintegrated and rehumanized in **union** with the **fleshy and spiritual** "new man **Jesus Christ**" (Eph 20.1, Eph 2:15). Ignatius's second concern is that our lives be *united* with **faith and love** (or his **faith***fulness* **and love**; see comments on Eph 20.1). This **fleshes** out our reception of the Eucharist. Thirdly, **and above all**, he longs for the **union** that the members of **the churches** can have through sharing in the **union of Jesus and the Father** (John 17:21–23, Eph 2.2, Mag 13.1–2). **By** continuing to share in their **union, we shall get to God.**

2

1. Since, then, I was counted worthy to see you through the persons of Damas, your God-worthy bishop, and the worthy presbyters Bassus and Apollonius, and my fellow slave the deacon Zotion—may I be the one to draw joy from him, because he freely submits himself to the bishop as to the grace of God, and to the council of presbyters as to the law of Jesus Christ.

EXHORTATION TO HONOR THE BISHOP

3

1. And it is right for you as well not to take advantage of the young age of your bishop. Instead, you should show him all the reverence that God the Father's power calls for. I have learned that even the holy presbyters have acted in the same way, not presuming upon his obvious youthfulness. Instead, they yield to him as to one wise in God, and yet not to him, but to the Father of Jesus Christ, the bishop of all.

2. Thus, for the honor of him who took pleasure in us, it is right to obey without any hypocrisy. For the point is not that someone is seeking to deceive this visible bishop, but that he is trying to cheat the invisible one. Now in such a case the reckoning is not with flesh, but with God, who knows our secrets.

4

1. It is right, then, not only to be called Christians, but to actually be such. By comparison, certain people call a man bishop, while doing everything without him. Such people do not appear to me to act in good conscience, since they do not assemble together in authorized meetings in keeping with what is commanded.

2

1. With exuberance—and in an incomplete sentence—Ignatius humbly calls **the deacon Zotion** his **fellow slave** in serving **Jesus Christ** (Eph 2.1, Phld 4.1, Sm 12.2). To bring **joy to** others, a Christian must **freely submit himself to the** leadership of his church (Heb 13:7, 17; for the exception, see Acts 5:27–29, Mart Pol 10.2). In so doing, he **submits himself to the grace of God and to Jesus Christ's** "perfect **law** of liberty" (Jas 1:25, Gal 6:2, Rom Sal, Eph 2.2, Tr 13.2). **Christ's law** liberates, unlike that of Moses (see 8–11), but the freedom he gives is not antinomian (Matt 5:17–20, Rom 8:1–5, Eph 9.2, Phld 1.2).

EXHORTATION TO HONOR THE BISHOP

3

1. By **as well** Ignatius indicates that they **should** "freely submit to" **Bishop Damas** like Deacon Zotion does (2.1). He then contrasts **taking advantage** with **showing reverence** and **the youthfulness of the bishop** with **God the Father's power.** They **should show reverence for** their **bishop by yielding to him** as the *saintly* **presbyters** do. Literally, **presbyter** (elder) means *older man.* Thus, *old* age **yields to** the wise **young bishop.** This is in keeping with Paul's admonition to Timothy (1 Tim 4:12).

2. By **honoring** the **bishop, we honor God.** Such **honor** must come from a heart that yields **obedience** with full consent, that is, **without hypocrisy** or *pretense.* Outward show might **deceive** the **bishop,** but it will not fool **God.** Hiding **secret**s can never **deceive him** (Eph 15.3, Phld 7.1, Sm 9.1, Phil 4.3).

4

1. Those who **call a man** pastor, **while doing everything without him,** are just like the **people** Ignatius describes as "deceiving the **bishop**" by their *"pretense"* (3.2). What they **do** (or *perform*) *apart from* **him** includes **meet**ing without **authorization** for worship, perhaps on the Sabbath (see 9.1). This is contrary to the apostolic **commandment:** "Let everything be done properly and in order" (1 Cor 14:40). Even today, there can be no Orthodox celebration of the Liturgy **without** a **bishop's authorization** (Sm 8.1).

THE TWO WAYS OF DEATH AND LIFE

5

1. Therefore, since our actions have their logical conclusion and there are two ways that lie before us simultaneously, namely death and life, each person shall in fact end up where he belongs.

2. For just as there are two types of coinage, the one God's, and the other the world's, and each of them has its own stamp impressed upon it, so the unbelievers bear the stamp of this world, while the faithful in love bear the stamp of God the Father through Jesus Christ. Unless through him we voluntarily embrace the dying that unites us to his passion, there is no living of him in us.

THE TWO WAYS OF DEATH AND LIFE

5

1. There are only **two ways** set **before us: death and life** (Deut 30:19, Ps 1:6; for more on the **two ways**, see Mag 5.2, 13.1; Did 1.1—6.2; Barn 18–21). There are no alternatives, no matter how many **ways** one might seek to escape the "fear of death" through the devil's illusions (Heb 2:14–15). One such illusion is reincarnation, which teaches there is no **end** to second chances (a doctrine clearly opposed in Heb 9:27–28, 12:16–17). **Therefore** points back to the earlier comparison between those who "show reverence" for their "bishop" (3.1), which **ends** in **life**, and those who "do everything without him" (4.1), which **ends** in **death**.

2. Here Ignatius depicts the "two ways" (5.1) as **two types of coinage**. In continuing the theme of "death and life" begun in 5.1, Ignatius shows how these **two** are both at work in "**the faithful** [who **live**] in love" (Wis 3:9; Wis 3:1–9 is read on the feast days of martyrs). **The faithful** can also be rendered *the believers*, whose **love**-filled **lives** stand in *marked* contrast to **the worldly unbelievers**. By **voluntarily dying** to sin now **in loving** union with **his passion, his** *suffering*, we have **Christ living in us**. As St. Paul said, "I have been crucified with **Christ**, and it is no longer I who **live**, but **Christ** who **lives in** me. And the **life** that I now **live in** the flesh, I **live** by faith, the faith that is in the Son of **God**, Who **loved** me and gave himself up for me" (Gal 2:20). **Through Christ living in us**, others will see **the stamp** (**the** *imprint* or *mark*) given to us that discloses "**the** *express image*" of **God the Father, Jesus Christ** (Heb 1:3, Tr Sal).

EXHORTATION TO UNITY

6

1. Since, then, in the persons mentioned above I have by faith looked on the whole community and loved it, I exhort you: eagerly exert effort to celebrate every service in divine harmony, with the bishop presiding in the place of God, the presbyters in the place of the council of the apostles, and the deacons, most sweet to me, being entrusted with the service of Jesus Christ, who before the ages was with the Father and appeared at the end.

2. Let all of you, then, take up the godly convictions and habits that you share in common and show one another respect. Indeed, let nobody view his neighbor in a merely human way. Rather, love each other constantly in Jesus Christ. Let there be nothing among you that will be able to divide you. Instead, be united with the bishop and with those who preside for an example and lesson of incorruptibility.

7

1. Therefore, just as the Lord did nothing without the Father—because of their being united—either by himself or through the apostles, in the same way you yourselves must do nothing without the bishop and the presbyters. And you must not try to make anything appear reasonable on your own. Instead, when you join together in the common assembly, have one prayer, one petition, one mind, one hope, in love, in blameless joy, which is Jesus Christ. Nothing is better than him.

EXHORTATION TO UNITY

6

1. **Eagerly exert effort** may also be translated *be diligent* or *eagerly strive,* both here and elsewhere. Christian **community** needs everyone's **efforts to celebrate every service in divine harmony** (*with one and the same godly mind*; Mag 15.1, Phld Sal; Tr 12.2). Each of us is to be an example of our **whole community.** When we assemble for the Eucharist in a Hierarchical Divine Liturgy, **the bishop presides in God's place** from his throne, **the presbyters** take **the apostles's place** gathered around the altar table, and **the deacons** (in Greek the same word means *servants*) **serve** as **Jesus Christ** did at the Last Supper (Tr 3.1, 2.2–3; Sm 8.1; Phld 8.1). **Christ appeared at the end**, that is, "in these last days" (Heb 1:1–2).

2. The "divine harmony" stressed in 6.1 comes from our **unity** in the Eucharist, over which our leaders **preside**. It is shown by **the godly convictions and habits that** we **share in common** (Pol 1.3). Because of our **common** life, we should **show one another respect** and **view** our **neighbor as Jesus Christ** does, rather than **in a merely human** (literally, *fleshy*) **way.** We should **let nothing divide** us from **one another** and our leaders (1 Thess 5:12–13). God has given them to us **for an example and lesson** on how to live an **incorruptible** life **in Jesus Christ** (Heb 13:7, 17).

7

1. By acting jointly with our leaders, we imitate our **Lord,** who acted jointly with his **Father** (John 5:19, 1 Cor 11:1). **On your own** (that is, *in isolation from the church*) **refers** to factions that would go their **own** way. If the Magnesians follow what *looks* **"reasonable"** to those people (Sm 9.1), they will "divide" themselves off (6.2) from **the one common assembly** and **join** in worship with heretics (Mag 8.1, Eph 5.2—7.1). To be **one** with **Jesus Christ** is to **have one prayer, one petition, one mind, one hope in love** and **blameless joy. When** we **join together** to celebrate the Eucharist, let us **joyfully** display our **unity** through **"one** temple, **one** altar, **one Jesus Christ,"** and **"one Father"** (7.2).

2. All of you must run together as into one temple of God, as to one altar, to one Jesus Christ, who came forth from one Father, while remaining turned toward only one, and then returned.

CHRISTIANITY SUPERSEDES JUDAISM

8

1. Do not be deluded by heterodox teachings and practices, nor by old fables, since they are useless. For if we still go on living in accordance with Judaism, we are admitting that we have not received grace.

2. Ignatius uses the word **as** before **one temple** and **one altar** because the Church has many **temples** (the traditional name for Orthodox houses of worship) and many **altars**, but they are all **one**. Upon the **one altar** is **Jesus Christ**, who offered himself to the **Father** once and for all (Heb 7:25–27, 10:9–14), but now offers himself as food for the faithful in the Eucharist (John 6:47–58). **Jesus Christ came forth from the one Father** for our salvation at his incarnation. He kept oriented **toward only one** throughout his earthly ministry, and afterward *went back* to him (John 20:17). The emphasis on **one** calls to mind the *Shema Israel*, which was very important to Second Temple Judaism: "Hear, O Israel, the Lord our God, the Lord is **one**" (Deut 6:4). The repeated use of **one** provides a transition to Ignatius's treatment of Judaism and Judaizers in Magnesia (8–11). The Hebrew word for **one** in the *Shema* can also mean *first* among several and so point to **God the Father** with his Word (8.2) and his Spirit (Sm Sal).

CHRISTIANITY SUPERSEDES JUDAISM

8

1. **Heterodox** can mean a *different glory* or a *different opinion* and can refer to *differences* in worship, **teachings, and practices** (see Sm 6.2). Ignatius had to combat all these, for they lead to each other. **The old fables** refer to **Judaism**'s erroneous rabbinic lore on the **Old** Testament (1 Tim 1:4, 4:6–7; Titus 3:9). They are **useless** because they lack the **grace** of Christ. (On **Judaism**, see Mag 8–11 and Phld 3–9, particularly Mag 8.2, Mag 10.3, and Phld 6.1.)

2. For the most divine prophets lived in accordance with Christ Jesus. Indeed this is why they were persecuted, for they were inspired by his grace in order that the disobedient might be fully convinced that there is one God who made himself manifest through Jesus Christ his Son. He is his Word who came forth from silence, who in every way well-pleased him who sent him.

9

1. If, then, those who used to conduct their lives in keeping with antiquated practices came to newness of hope, no longer keeping the Sabbath, but living in accordance with the Lord's Day—on which day our life also dawned through him and his death (though some deny it); and through this mystery we laid hold of believing, and because of it we patiently endure, in order that we may prove to be disciples of Jesus Christ, our only Teacher—

2. By using the word for **divine** that refers to the **divine** nature, Ignatius indicates **the prophets** were already "partaking of God" (Eph 4.2, 2 Pet 1:4). This was because they **lived in accordance with Christ Jesus**, instead of "Judaism" (8.1, Phld 6.1). **Through Jesus Christ, the one God** has manifested himself (made himself *appear*; Eph 19.3). **Persecution** of those who are **full** of **grace** may result in the gospel **fully convincing** those who are still **disobedient** and *unpersuaded* Jews (on **fully convinced**, see comments on 11.1). Without the "**grace**" of God (8.1) and his **Christ**, they are left to a preincarnate **silence** that will not accept anything "new" from the **one God** (Mag 9.1, 7.2; Eph 19.2, 20.1; Mag 10.2). Beyond his concern with Judaizers, Ignatius saw in the **persecution of the prophets** a harbinger of his own **persecution** and surely hoped that his martyrdom would **convince** the pagans of the **one God who** *appeared* **through Jesus Christ, his Word** (*Logos*) **who came forth from silence** (for citations on the *Logos*, see Sm Sal; on **silence**, see Eph 19.1).

9

1. **This mystery** points to their baptism (Tr 2.3, 2.1; Eph 12.2). When the Jews turned to Christ under the preaching of the apostles, a **new day dawned** (indeed *arose*), as they were united to **his death** and initiated into a **life** of **believing** (see Phil 4.2). The Jews who **denied** that **life dawned** because of the **death** of our **Lord** were like the Docetists who "**denied**" the physical "passion" of **Christ** (Sm 5.1–3; for more on the Docetists, who were a Gnostic group, see Tr 5–11; Sm 2–7, 13.2). **We**, both Jew and Gentile, who have been initiated into the Paschal **mystery** of **Christ's death** and resurrection (Sm 5.3), now **conduct** our **lives in** the light of **the Lord's Day**, Sunday, the day on which he *arose* (Rev 1:10, Did 14.1). Christian **disciples** do not listen to rabbis or their **disciples**, the Judaizers, but rather to **Jesus Christ, our only Teacher.**

2. how shall we be able to live without him, when even the prophets, who were his disciples in the Spirit, were expecting him as their Teacher? And for this reason, when he came, he for whom they waited righteously raised them from the dead.

10

1. Let us not, then, be numb to his kindness, for if he should imitate the way we act, we shall no longer exist. Therefore, since we are his disciples, let us learn how to live in accordance with Christianity. For whoever is called by any other name than this is not of God.

2. Put aside, then, the bad leaven, which has grown old and sour, and be changed into the new leaven, which is Jesus Christ. Be salted with him, in order that none of you become rotten, since, in that case, you will be exposed by the smell.

3. It is absurd to profess Jesus Christ and practice Judaism. For Christianity did not come to believe in Judaism, but Judaism in Christianity. Into it every tongue that has put its faith in God has been gathered together.

2. We, like **the prophets,** are **disciples** of the same **Teacher,** Jesus Christ. We cannot **live without him:** "To whom shall we go?"—for **he** has "the words of eternal **life**" (John 6:68). **The prophets waited righteously,** that is, with "a **righteous**ness not of the law but through faith" (Phil 3:9). And **they** waited *rightly,* for it was *right* that **they waited for** the coming **Teacher** about whom Moses had prophesied (Deut 18:15–22). Upon his death Christ entered Hades; **and when** he rose, he **raised from the dead** the saints who died before him, including his Forerunner, John the Baptist, as well as all **the** other **prophets** (1 Pet 3:19, 4:6; Matt 27:50–54; Phil 1.2; Frag 28).

10

1. The Greek word translated **numb** is related to our medical term *anesthesia.* Here it refers to any *lack of feeling* on our part for the **kindness** displayed by "his death" and our "new **life**" (9.1). In 10.1–3, Ignatius is appealing to those **Christians** who might be confused about Judaism. They **are disciples** of **Christ,** not of the Judaizers, and should follow **Christianity,** rather than Judaism (the **other name**), which **is not of God** in its post-**Christian** form (8.1, 10.3; Phld 6.1). Here we find the first written instance of the word **Christianity.**

2. **The leaven** of Moses once was good, but now is **bad,** having **grown old and sour** (1 Cor 5:6–8; Mag 9.1; Heb 8:13; Matt 13:33, 52). **Now** Christians must **be changed into the new leaven, Jesus Christ,** so that we may grow in him. **Christ** is the **salt** for our self-offering (Lev 2:13, 2 Chr 13:5, Matt 5:13, Mark 9:49–50, Col 4:6). By being **salted** with him, we avoid **becoming rotten** (*going bad* or *getting corrupted;* on our need for *incorruptibility,* see Eph 17.1).

3. St. Ignatius asserts the preeminence of **Christianity:** what first-century **Judaism** had to offer to the whole world has now been fulfilled in **Christianity** (Matt 5:17). This is in keeping with his earlier statement that **Jesus Christ** had "discipled the prophets" (9.2). What passes for **Judaism** in Ignatius's day and ours is a "heterodox" development that "went *bad*" after rejecting **Jesus Christ** (8.1, 10.2). **Christianity** is for the Gentiles, as well as the Jews, and represents a reversal of the Tower of Babel: in **Christianity,** "**every** nation and **tongue**" are "**gathered together**" "**into** the house of the Lord" (Isa 66:18–20, Eph 2:14–16).

FINAL EXHORTATIONS

11

1. Now I write these things, my beloved ones, not because I know that some of you are so disposed, but because, as one less than you, I want to protect you in advance. Do not get snagged on the fishhooks of vainglory, but instead be fully convinced by experience of the birth and the passion and the resurrection that took place during the time when Pontius Pilate was governor. For these events were actually and assuredly accomplished by Jesus Christ, our hope. From this hope may it be granted that none of you ever be turned aside.

12

1. May I draw joy from you in every way, if only I be worthy. For even though I am in chains, I am nothing compared to a single one of you who are at liberty. I know that you are not puffed up, for you have Jesus Christ within yourselves. Moreover, whenever I praise you, I know that you shake your heads in shame, as it is written, "The righteous man is his own accuser."

FINAL EXHORTATIONS

11

1. The Magnesians were in danger of **being turned aside** from right **glory** (*orthodoxy*) and **getting** *hooked* **on** Jewish **vainglory** (*kenodoxy, empty glory*; Phld 1.1, Phil 2:3; on "cliquish ambition," see Phld 8.2, Phil 2:3; on Christ's *kenotic* "self-*emptying*," see Phil 2:7). St. Ignatius models humility as a way to avoid this by saying he is **less than**. **Vainglory** leads one to be "deluded by heterodoxy" (a different kind of **glory**; 8.1, Ag Heresies 4.26.2) and can end in us losing **Christ**. **Fully convinced by experience** is in the Greek perfect tense and can also be translated *filled full to overflowing*. So the safe path to **being fully convinced of** what **Christ accomplished by his birth, passion, and resurrection** is to *fully partake* of them **experientially** (Phld Sal, Sm 1.1, Pol 6.1). Orthodox strive to know **Christ** in this way by their walking in faith and love and *participating* in the Church's sacraments, prayers, services, and annual cycle of fasts and feasts (Phil 7.2—8.1).

12

1. The Magnesians are not **puffed up** (that is, *haughty*) when **praised** (1 Cor 8:1–4, 13:4). They live like people who **have within** themselves **Jesus Christ**, who stays far away from the *haughty* (Ps 137/138:6). Instead of being "snagged on [Jewish] vainglory" (11.1), they humbly **shake** their **heads in shame, accusing** themselves and saying no to human flattery (see Prov 18:17 LXX),. This keeps them from "thinking" of themselves "more highly than" they "ought" (Rom 12:3).

13

1. Strive eagerly, then, to be firmly grounded in the precepts of the Lord and the apostles. That way, in everything you ever do, you may prosper in flesh and spirit, in faith and love, in the Son and the Father and in the Spirit, at the beginning and at the end, along with your most right worthy bishop, your council of presbyters, that worthily woven spiritual crown, and the godly deacons.

2. Freely submit yourselves to the bishop and to one another, as Jesus Christ did to the Father and as the apostles did to Christ and to the Father, that there may be a union that is both physical and spiritual.

REQUEST FOR PRAYER AND FAREWELL

14

1. Recognizing that you are full of God, I have only exhorted you briefly. Remember me in your prayers—that I may attain to God—and the Church that is in Syria as well, from which I am not worthy to be called. For I am in need of your prayer and love that are united in God, in order that the Church that is in Syria may be counted worthy of being refreshed with dew through your church.

13

1. Ignatius utilizes Psalm 1 about "the man" who follows **the precepts** for God's "way" of life, and so is "blessed" with both *physical* (**fleshy**) and **spiritual "prosperity"** (1:1, 3, 6; on the two ways of "death and life," see Mag 5.1–2). By **the precepts of the Lord** and his **apostles**, Ignatius may have in mind *The Gospel according to Matthew* and Paul's epistles (see Acts 16:4 where the Greek word for **precepts** refers to the written *decisions* of the Jerusalem Council recorded in Acts 15:23–31; also see Phld 8.2). They are to be followed, not Moses. The pairing **in the Son and the Father and in the Spirit** is parallel to the pairs surrounding it (see Eph 9.1 on the ministry of the Trinity toward us). The first three pairs listed here are similar to those in Magnesians 1.2 on "union," and they are in the same order.

2. **Submission** is **to** everyone, not just **the bishop** (Eph 5:21, 1 Pet 5:5, Phil 10.2, 1 Clem 37.5—38.1). Our patterns for **submission** are **Jesus Christ and the apostles.** "As a man of flesh" (Sm 3.3, Eph 7.2), **Christ** is still in **submission to the Father** (1 Cor 15:24–28). So also are **the apostles,** who are now alive with **Christ** before the throne of God (Phld 5.1). Like them, our goal is **union of** *flesh* (our *outward,* **physical** *life*) **and spirit** (our *inward life of the heart*), so that everything may become "**spiritual** in Jesus Christ" (Eph 8.2, Mag 1.2). This requires an *outward, external* Church *unity,* not merely an amorphous, *internal* **spiritual union** of believers. Proper **submission** within our church community brings us into **union** with the Holy Trinity: **Christ, the Father,** "**and the Spirit**" (13.1). Many manuscripts include "and to the Spirit" after **and to the Father.**

REQUEST FOR PRAYER AND FAREWELL

14

1. These believers **are full of God** because they are "**fully** *partaking* of the birth, passion, and resurrection" of Jesus Christ (11.1). Ignatius's requests for **prayer** are usually in the singular, probably having in mind our **united prayer** during the Liturgy. Here he has two **needs** and so two **prayers:** that he **attain to God** through his coming martyrdom and that **the Church in Syria be refreshed with dew through** the corporate **prayer** of the Magnesian **church** (on **dew,** see Num 11:9, Judg 6:36–40, Ps 132/133:3; on "**the Church that is in Syria,**" see Eph 21.2).

15

1. The Ephesians embrace you from Smyrna. From there also I am writing you. Like you, they are here for the glory of God. Together with Polycarp, the bishop of the Smyrnaeans, they have refreshed me in every way. And the rest of the churches embrace you as well in honor of Jesus Christ. May you fare well in divine harmony, you who possess by acquisition an inseparable spirit, which is Jesus Christ.

15

1. The Magnesians are **there** through their delegation (2.1). Ignatius links **divine harmony** (6.1) to **an inseparable spirit** (or *Spirit*) that they have **acquired** (Pol 1.3). What is **inseparable** cannot be separated from God. This accords with the epistle's theme of unity. A church that has **acquired** an **inseparable spirit** is like **Jesus Christ**, "our **inseparable** life" (Eph 3.2). To **acquire an inseparable spirit** one must **acquire** *the* **inseparable Spirit**. St. Seraphim of Sarov says, "The true aim of our Christian life consists in the **acquisition** of the Holy **Spirit**" (Convers). Whenever Ignatius uses **which is**, he is making a connection between what he mentions first and what follows, leaving it to his audience to make one or more connections. So if **spirit** be taken as **Spirit**, then the Holy **Spirit** and **Jesus Christ** would be seen as **inseparable**, while remaining two distinct persons in the Holy Trinity (cf. 2 Cor 3:15–18).

The Epistle of St. Ignatius
to the Trallians

CONTENTS

SALUTATION

Ignatius the God-bearer to the holy church that is gathered at Tralles in Asia. You are beloved of God, the Father of Jesus Christ, and are elect and God-worthy. And you are at peace in flesh and spirit by the passion of Jesus Christ, who is our hope through the resurrection that joins us to him. Your church I also embrace in God's fullness in an apostolic character, and I bid you abundant greetings.

GRATITUDE FOR BISHOP POLYBIUS AND THE CHURCH

1

1. I know that you have a mind free from blame and unwavering in endurance. This is not from rote habit, but by nature. Polybius, your bishop, showed me this when he was here in Smyrna by the will of God and Jesus Christ. And by the way that he congratulated me, a chained criminal in Christ Jesus, I beheld your whole community in him.

2. As a consequence, I received your godly affection through him and offered glorious praise that I found you to be—as I knew you were—imitators of God.

SALUTATION

Tralles lay about eighteen miles northeast of Magnesia in a lush agricultural region located in the lower valley of the Maeander River. The river's winding back and forth has given us our word *meander*. The word for **character** can also be rendered *stamp* or *exact imprint* (on Christ as the *exact imprint* of the Father, see Heb 1:3). Ignatius has the **character** of apostolic authenticity because he is **God-bearer** and comes "in faith and in love" (8.1, 2.1, 6.1; Mag 5.2). He desires the *stamp* of **apostolic** likeness that *suffering*, martyrdom, and fully attaining to God will bring (12.2–3, 13.3; about the Apostle Paul's *sufferings*, see 2 Cor 6:3–10, 11:23–30). Meanwhile, **the passion of Jesus Christ** brings peace, both *outwardly* (**in flesh**) and *inwardly* (**in spirit**), to his **church**. In addition, we have **Christ** as **our hope through the resurrection that joins us to him**: starting with our baptism, continuing on from day to day, and finally in our rising up at his return—if we "keep on relying on him" (Tr 9.2, Rom 6:1–16).

GRATITUDE FOR BISHOP POLYBIUS AND THE CHURCH

1

1. The faithful in Tralles act out of their "renewed" **nature** in Christ (Col 3:10, 2 Pet 1:4–8) by partaking of his divine **nature**, not just **from** a **rote habit** of external virtue. Ignatius knows this by **Polybius's** example. **In him** he sees their **whole community** (Eph 1.3, Mag 6.1).

2. Ignatius may be **offering glorious praise** to **God**, Bishop Polybius, or both. The faithful **imitate God** out of their "righteous nature" (Eph 1.1, Tr 1.1). By his continuing to **imitate God**, Polybius has come to possess "a blameless and unwavering mind" (Tr 1.1, Eph 5:1, Pol 1.1).

SUBMISSION TO THE BISHOP AND HIS CLERGY

2

1. For whenever you freely submit yourselves to the bishop as to Jesus Christ, it is evident to me that you are not living the way people typically do, but the way Jesus Christ wants us to. He died for our sakes in order that, by putting your faith in his death, you may escape dying.

2. It is essential, therefore, in keeping with your current practice, that you do nothing without the bishop. But you must also freely submit yourselves to the council of presbyters as to the apostles of Jesus Christ. He is our hope, and if on him we spend our lives, in him we shall be found.

3. Now it is also necessary that those who are deacons of the mysteries of Jesus Christ be pleasing to everyone in every way. For they are not just servers of food and drink, but rather assistants of God's Church. Therefore, they must guard themselves against accusations as if they were fire.

3

1. Likewise let all of you show reverence for the deacons as you do for Jesus Christ, even as you also show reverence for the bishop because he is a type of the Father and for the presbyters as the council of God and the apostles's band. Without these, no group is called a church.

2. I am convinced that you think the same about these, for I received the model example of your love—and still have it with me—in your bishop. His very demeanor holds a great lesson, and his meekness is powerful. I think even the atheists respect him.

SUBMISSION TO THE BISHOP AND HIS CLERGY

2

1. **Freely submitting** ourselves to our pastor **as to Jesus Christ** is "essential" (2.2) to our **living Christ's way** and **escaping** spiritual **dying**, both now and in the age to come (for more on the necessity of **submission**, see Heb 13:7, 17, as well as comments on Eph 2.2). We either yield our wills to God or pride reigns and we end up **living the way people typically do, putting** their **faith in** themselves and spiritually **dying**. By using the pronoun **your,** attention is redirected to their own baptism into **Christ's death** and to their personal commitment to **live** as Christians (Rom 6:3–13).

2. For **presbyter,** English-speaking countries have often used the word *priest,* which comes from *preost,* Old English for **presbyter. Our hope** to **be found** in **Jesus Christ** depends on how **we spend our lives:** Are we "running" in good faith with our leaders (13.2; Eph 4.1; Pol 6.1, 7.3)?

3. **Deacons** and **servers** translate the same Greek word. While **deacons** did regularly distribute **food and drink** (and one meaning of **deacon** is *waiter*), their most important **service** was **assisting God's Church** in public worship: in **the mysteries of Jesus Christ** (the sacraments of baptism and Eucharist) and **in the** preaching **of** the word (Eph 12.2, Phld 11.1, 1 Cor 4:1).

3

1. We are to **show the deacons the** same **reverence** we **show** *to* **Jesus Christ** and all his other ministers. In the **churches** Ignatius visited, he clearly saw a **bishop** with **presbyters** and **deacons,** and the Orthodox **Church** of our day has the same clergy. By the third century, we find one **bishop** per city overseeing the **presbyters** who pastored the congregations there.

2. **These** refers to the positions of "**bishop,** presbyter, and deacon" (3.1). **Meekness is** very **powerful,** for it is "the **meek**" who "shall inherit the earth" (Matt 5:5, Ps 36/37:11, 4.2, Eph 10.2). The Christians were name-called "**atheists**" (*people without gods*) for not believing in the Roman deities (Mart Pol 3.2, 9.2). Here Ignatius refers to the pagans in Tralles as **atheists.** If **even** they **respect Bishop** Polybius, he is indeed a worthy man.

HUMILITY AND SPIRITUAL WARFARE

3. Though I could write more pointedly on his behalf, I refrain out of love for you. I did not suppose that I, being a convict, should give you orders like an apostle.

4

1. I have many divine thoughts, but I take the measure of myself lest I perish through boasting. For the present it is far better for me to be fearful and not give heed to those who try to puff me up, for those who speak to me are flogging me.

2. Yes, I do love suffering, but whether I am worthy I do not know, for envy—though not apparent to many—wages war against me all the more. Therefore, I need meekness, by which the ruler of this age is destroyed.

5

1. Am I not able to write you about heavenly things? Of course I can, but I am afraid to, lest I do harm to you who are just babes. So bear with me, lest you be choked by what you cannot swallow.

HUMILITY AND SPIRITUAL WARFARE

3. Ignatius does not claim the authority of **an apostle**, though he clearly believes he has received authority from them—after all, he calls the presbyters "the apostles's band" (3.1). Rather, it is **out of** humble **love** that he **refrains** from **giving orders** (Rom 4.3, Eph 3.1). He is not one to shy away from telling his audience what they **should** do; however, his concern here is to model "meekness" like their bishop (3.2), in order to avoid "boasting" (4.1) on his part or theirs (4.1—5.2).

4

1. Ignatius wants to emulate Bishop Polybius's "powerful meekness" (3.2) and avoid being **puffed up** with pride. He expects to be **flogged** by the Romans both now and later, so he determines **for the present** to "meekly" (3.2) endure being **flogged** by the praises of his enticers, lest he **perish through boasting** at this time or in the arena (4.2, 3.2; Pol 5.2; Mart Pol 4.1).

2. Ignatius **loves suffering** because he **loves** *the* Lord's *passion* (Rom 4.3, Pol 7.1, Jas 1:2). **But** because he **knows** himself, he questions *if* he is **worthy** to share in the Lord's *passion* through **suffering** as a martyr. Here **envy** is either the **envy** of **the ruler**—or the *envious* **ruler**—**of this age**, who **wages war** to destroy the saint (Rom 5.3; Matt 27:18; Acts 17:5–8; Wis 2:24; 1 Clem 3.4, 4.7, 5.2, 9.1; Mart Pol 2.4, 17.1–2). Even though "the devil prowls around like a roaring lion" and later on lions will "devour" St. Ignatius, through **meekness** this *unassuming and strong* **martyr** shall best **the ruler of this age** (1 Pet 5:8, Tr 8.1, Eph 10.2).

5

1. Ignatius, as a wise pastor, is careful not to feed any "meat" to **babes** in the faith, **lest** they **choke** (1 Cor 3:1–4, Heb 5:12–14). But his chief concern is *infantile* spiritual pride fed by the Gnostics (here through 7.1).

2. For even in my own case, though I am in chains, and though I can see into heavenly things—the positions assigned to angels and the formations of the princely powers, things both seen and unseen—I am not yet a disciple because of this. For we lack many things, lest we lack God.

AVOIDING HERESY AND HERETICS

6

1. Therefore, I exhort you (yet not I, but the love of Jesus Christ): avail yourselves of only Christian fare, and avoid any strange plant, which is heresy.

2. These people, while pretending to be trustworthy, mix Jesus Christ with themselves. It is like those who administer a deadly drug with honeyed wine. The unsuspecting victim gladly takes it, and thus with wicked pleasure drinks down death.

7

1. Therefore, be on your guard against such people. And this will be possible for you, so long as you are not puffed up and remain inseparable from Jesus Christ, the bishop, and the injunctions of the apostles.

2. Ignatius mocks the Gnostic claims to special spiritual knowledge of **heavenly things** involving **the powers** of the zodiac, that is, **the positions assigned to angels and the** *conjunctions* **of the princely powers** (Sm 6.1). He says a **chained** convict **can see** as much. But this supposed **seeing** (*noetic perception*) does not make one **a disciple** (Eph 1.2, 3.1; Rom 4.2, 5.1, 5.3; Pol 7.1). What **can** is really **seeing** what we **lack** by means of the increasingly purified eye of our heart and letting this **lack** propel us **into God,** *that* **we** *not* **lack** him.

AVOIDING HERESY AND HERETICS

6

1. A **heresy** is a *faction or sect with different opinions* that grows in **plants** (communities) that are **strange** (or *alien*) and *different* from what is healthy (11.1–2; Eph 6.2, 10.3; Mart Pol Mosc 22.2; 1 Cor 11:18–19).

2. Those "planting heresy" (6.1) are full of **themselves with** a bit of **Jesus mixed** in. Under the guise of presenting—and representing—**Jesus Christ,** they tempt **unsuspecting** people with **wicked pleasures** and poison them to **death** (Eph 16.2). Such a draft is the opposite of "the medicine of immortality" that "enables living in **Jesus Christ** forever" (Eph 20.2)!

7

1. One cannot "avoid" (6.1)—or be safely **guarded** from—**such** heretics while being **puffed up** with pride. Such pride **separates** us **from Christ** and his ministers. **The injunctions** (or *orders*) **of the apostles** may include their instructions for worship which **the bishop** implements "within the altar" (7.2, Mag 4.1).

2. The one within the altar is pure, but the one outside the altar is not pure. This means that whoever performs anything apart from the bishop and the council of presbyters and the deacons is not pure in conscience.

8

1. I am not aware of any such thing among you, but I am protecting you in advance as my beloved ones, because I foresee the traps of the devil. As for you, then, make meekness your own and renew yourselves in faith, which is the flesh of the Lord, and in love, which is the blood of Jesus Christ.

2. Let none of you hold a grudge against his neighbor. Give no opportunity to the pagans, lest the godly majority of your community be slandered on account of a few fools. For woe to the one through whom "my name is" vainly "blasphemed" among any of them.

2. A **pure conscience** comes through worthily receiving his most **pure** body and blood from his authorized ministers. The Trallians have "an **altar to eat**" from that the heretics do not (Heb 13:10, Eph 5.2–3, Sm 7.1). Impurity is the root of heresy. Even if the Docetists do **perform** the Eucharist, they do not actually *celebrate* it (7.2; Eph 4.2, 5.2). **Perform** means *do, act,* or *practice* and is the same word usually rendered in this translation as *celebrate* when the Eucharist is being *celebrated* by those in communion with the apostles and their successors, such as St. Ignatius and St. Polycarp. The key is not to *act* **apart from the bishop** and his clergy. We should always get our pastor's blessing.

8

1. How do we **renew** our energy? By being **meek**—rather than "begrudging" (8.2, Eph 10.2) and "deadly" (11.1)—and by gathering together to receive in the Eucharist **the flesh and blood of the Lord Jesus Christ**, which are the embodiment and source of **faith and love** (see Mag 15.1 for Ignatius's use of **which is**). By speaking of **Christ's flesh and blood**, Ignatius supported his insistence on **Christ's** humanity, which the Docetists denied.

2. Ignatius is referencing Isa 52:5 LXX, where God's "**name**" is said to be "**blasphemed** among the *nations*" (also translated *the Gentiles*, **pagans**, or *heathen*; Polycarp quotes from this scripture in Phil 10.2–3). The same Greek word means to **slander** people and to **blaspheme** God. How quickly charges of **slander** and **blasphemy** are made whenever we **hold** anything **against** our **neighbor**. Ignatius is seeking to avoid any scandalous interaction between the Christians and the Docetists in Tralles, and **the pagans** might consider the Docetists to be the "**neighbors**" of the Christians (Luke 10:29–37; 1 Clem 1.1, 47.6–7). Hence Ignatius starts the next sentence with "So" (9.1).

CHRIST'S REAL DEATH AND RESURRECTION

9

1. So act like a deaf-mute whenever anyone should speak to you apart from Jesus Christ, who was of the lineage of David and the Son of Mary. He really was born, both ate and drank, really was prosecuted under Pontius Pilate, and really was crucified and died, while those in heaven and on earth and under the earth looked on.

2. Moreover, he really was raised up from the dead by his Father raising him up. In keeping with this same pattern, his Father shall likewise also raise up in Christ Jesus those of us who keep on relying on him. Without him we have no real living.

10

1. But if as some atheists—that is, unbelievers—say, that he seemed to suffer (while they themselves are the ones doing the seeming!), why am I myself in chains? And why do I also wish to fight with wild beasts? If what they say is so, there is no point in my dying. Furthermore, I am then bearing false witness against the Lord.

11

1. Flee, then, the wicked offshoots that give birth to death-bearing fruit. If anyone should taste it, he dies right then and there, for these are not the Father's plantings.

CHRIST'S REAL DEATH AND RESURRECTION

9

1. If **anyone should** *say* something **to you** that does not come from **Jesus Christ, act like a deaf-mute**: neither give him heed, nor **speak** like you agree with him (Eph 16.2). Ignatius is concerned with **anyone** who would try to falsify **Christ's** *true* humanity, particularly the Docetists. **Prosecute** is the legal meaning of *persecute*. **Those in heaven** (the cosmic powers) could **look on** at **Christ's** judgment and death because he was a **real** man in **real** flesh.

2. In order for us to be **raised up by** the **Father**, we must **keep on relying on** (*trusting in*) **Christ Jesus**. Then we **shall** have a sure hope to be **raised** in the **same** way that **Christ** was (Rom 6:4–5, 1 Cor 6:14). **Real living** is only found **in him** (Eph 11.1, Mag 5.2), both now and in the resurrection to come.

10

1. The **atheists** here are not **unbelievers** in general, but specifically Ignatius's *faithless* heretical opponents, the Docetists. Their name means those who **believe** in **seeming**, in reference to their **belief** in Jesus Christ's **seeming**, but not real, humanity. As ones who do not **believe** in the really born, crucified, and raised man Jesus Christ (8.1, 9.1–2), they say **he seemed to be suffering,** but actually was not. Ignatius, however, says **they are the ones doing the seeming**, who **seem** to be Christians, but really are not (cf. Rom 3.2).

11

1. These heretics are fake **offshoots**. Like with the forbidden tree in paradise, the one who **tastes** the **fruit** of these **offshoots dies**. For none of them is an **offshoot** of the one tree of life which **the Father planted** (Matt 15:13). Earlier, Ignatius had spoken of the **wicked** heretics's deceptive and lethal ways in terms of proffering a "deadly drug" hidden in "honeyed wine" (6.2).

2. For if they were, they would be appearing as branches of the cross and their fruit would be imperishable. Through it, by his passion, he summons you who are his members. Now a head cannot be born by itself without its body's members, since God promises union, which is himself.

FINAL EXHORTATIONS, REQUEST FOR PRAYER, AND FAREWELL

12

1. I embrace you from Smyrna together with the churches of God that are present with me. In every way they have refreshed me, both in flesh and in spirit.

2. My chains—which I carry about for the sake of Jesus Christ as I ask to attain to God—exhort you to continue in your likemindedness and corporate prayer. For it is right for each and every one of you, and especially the presbyters, to refresh the bishop to the honor of the Father of Jesus Christ and the honor of the apostles.

3. I request in love that you listen to me, lest I become a witness against you by having written you. And pray for me also, for I need the love that is coming from you in the mercy of God, that I may be counted worthy to attain my pending lot, lest I be found to be a failure after testing.

13

1. The love of the Smyrnaeans and of the Ephesians embraces you. Remember in your prayers the Church that is in Syria, of which I am not worthy to be called a member, since I am the least of them.

2. **The cross** is the true "planting" (11.1) and tree of life, and we are its **branches** (John 15:1–8). We are proved so by our **imperishable** (*incorruptible*) **fruit.** Our **summons** to **union** with **God** only comes **through it (the cross) by** Christ's **passion** (*suffering*). There was no other way but **the cross** for him, our **Head**; nor is there for us, **his Body.** As the **head appears** first at birth, and then the **body**, so our **Head**, having passed through death, offers his **members** upon their deaths eternal comm**union** with **God**, the Trinity, one in essence and undivided (see Eph 14.1 on "having God").

FINAL EXHORTATIONS, REQUEST
FOR PRAYER, AND FAREWELL

12

1. **Both in flesh and in spirit** refers to the totality of his *physical* and *spiritual* needs. **The churches are present** through their representatives (1.1–2).

2. Ignatius's **chains exhort** the Trallians **to continue** (*stay steadfast*) **in corporate prayer** (literally, *the with-one-another* **prayer**) for him **to attain to God** in the arena at Rome. **Likemindedness** is *unanimity or sameness of mind* (Eph 4.1, 13.1; Phld 11.2; Mag 6.1). **Presbyters** are to lead in providing **refreshing** hospitality (Phil 6.1).

3. **Witness** and *martyr* are the same word in Greek. The Trallians **need** the *martyr* Ignatius to come before God as **a witness** on their behalf. **To** *obtain* his **pending lot**, he needs **the love that is coming from** them to him through their "corporate **prayer**" (12.2).The **lot** that is *hanging* in the balance is whether Ignatius will **attain to God** by being a faithful *martyr* or whether he will **fail.** (For more on his **attaining** to **God** through his **lot** of *martyrdom*, see Rom 1.1–2 and Phld 5.1. For more on Polycarp's **lot**, see Mart Pol 6.2.) **A failure** can also be translated *disqualified* or *a reject* (1 Cor 9:27).

13

1. In asking for **prayers**, instead of **prayer** (see Mag 14.1, Eph 11.2), Ignatius may be thinking of **prayers** for all the **churches**, including that of Antioch, that are part of **the Church that is in Syria** (see Rom 2.2, Eph 21.2, Rom 9.1).

2. May you fare well in Jesus Christ, staying in submission to the bishop as you do to God's commandment—and likewise also to the council of presbyters. And each one of you must love everyone else with an undivided heart.

3. My very spirit is purified for you, not only now, but also whenever I may attain to God. For I am still in peril, but the Father is faithful in Jesus Christ to fulfill my request and yours. May we be found blameless in him.

2. To **fare well**, we must freely choose to **stay in submission to the bishop and presbyters** (2.1–2, Phil 5.3). The faithful **stay**, while those who follow erring leaders leave for differing groups, which Ignatius calls "the devil's planting" (Eph 10.3; Tr 6.1, 11.1; Phld 3.1; Acts 20:28–30). When **each one of** us has **an undivided, loving heart** for **everyone else** (Eph 14.1, Phld 6.2), **division** and heresy can be avoided.

3. **Now** in this life—and for later on **whenever** he has **attained to God**—Ignatius **is purifying** his **own spirit**, so that his self-offering can profit others (Eph 8.1, 18.1, 21.1; Sm 10.2; Pol 2.3, 6.1; Ignatius Intro, 5–6). This profiting of others will include his participation in the ongoing ministry of the saints in heaven for the faithful on earth. As a **purified** saint, he will be offering up prayer that they may **be found blameless in Christ. Whenever** indicates a degree of conditionality: while Ignatius hopes to **attain**, it is not for certain that he will, and he might not (Eph 12.2). So, at the time of his writing, he is **still in peril** (Eph 12.1) and needs their prayer to see him through to a faithful martyrdom (12.3). We find the same mindset in St. Paul when he writes, "That I may know him [**Christ**] and the power of his resurrection and may share in his sufferings. . .that, *if* somehow, I may **attain** to the resurrection from the dead" (Phil 3:10–11). Paul handled the uncertainty of the *if* in this way: "Not that I have already received or am now perfected [see Phld 5.1], but I press on, seeing *if* I may take hold of that for which I was also taken hold of by **Christ Jesus**. . .Forgetting what lies behind and straining forward to what lies ahead, I keep pressing on toward the goal for the prize of the upward call of **God** in **Christ Jesus**" (Phil 3:12–14; see Eph 12.2 on **attain**, Pol 1.2 on "press on," and Pol 1.3 on "strain").

The Epistle of St. Ignatius
to the Romans

CONTENTS

SALUTATION

Ignatius the God-bearer to the Church that has been granted mercy in the majesty of the Father Most High and Jesus Christ his only Son. By the will of him who willed all that exists, yours is a Church that is beloved and enlightened in accordance with the faithfulness and love of Jesus Christ our God. You who preside in the area of the region of the Romans are God-worthy, honorworthy, blessingworthy, praiseworthy, successworthy, and purityworthy. As ones presiding over charity, under the law of Christ, and named after the Father, I embrace you in the name of Jesus Christ, the Father's Son—you who are united in flesh and spirit to every commandment of his, having been filled with God's grace without wavering and filtered clear of every alien hue. Abundant greetings without blame in Jesus Christ our God.

IGNATIUS'S DESIRE TO BE UNHINDERED

1

1. Since by praying to God I have succeeded in seeing your God-worthy faces, I have as a result asked to receive still more. For I hope to embrace you as a chained criminal in Christ Jesus, if only it be God's will for me to be counted worthy of making it to the end.

2. For the beginning is, indeed, auspicious, provided I obtain grace to receive my lot unhindered. For I fear your charity, lest it be the thing that does me wrong. For it is easy for you to do what you want, but it is difficult for me to attain to God, unless you spare me.

SALUTATION

Rome was the capital of the empire. There Peter and Paul were martyred, and to the **Church** there Paul sent his *Epistle to the **Romans***. **Being enlightened** refers to baptism. **The Father and his Son** share one **majesty**. **Faithfulness and love of** can also be translated *faith in and love for* (Eph 20.1, Mag 1.2). Some scholars think that **Rome** had no overarching bishop, just one who corresponded on behalf of all the bishops pastoring the congregations that comprised the **Church** at **Rome** (contrast 4.1 with 9.3, and see Eph 21.2, Tr 13.1, Ag Heresies 3.3.3; on the three orders of ministry, see 1 Clem 40.1–5, Tr 3.1). In any case, Ignatius says nothing about any **area** beyond **Rome** where a bishop might **preside**, but points out where **the Church of Rome** does **preside** (or *is preeminent*): in the **area of charity**. He fears their **charity** may prevent his martyrdom (1.2, 2.1). **United in flesh and spirit to every commandment** refers to their total obedience (on **the law of Christ**, see Mag 2.1), as does **filled with God's grace without wavering** (or *discord*). **God's filtering** helped **clear the Church of** every *shade* of **alien** (or *strange*) heresy and division (Phld 3.1, 3; Tr 6.1).

IGNATIUS'S DESIRE TO BE UNHINDERED

1

1. Ignatius has *obtained* the opportunity to **see** the faithful in Rome. Next he wants **to embrace** them in person, and then **be counted worthy of making it to** martyrdom for **Christ Jesus**. More literally, **making it to the end** is *attaining* or *reaching the goal*.

2. If Ignatius's journey to Rome "ends" up (1.1) being a pilgrimage to martyrdom, then **the beginning** of his passage—his arrest, enchainment, and subsequent movement—will have been **auspicious**: a *favorable, well-arranged*, sign of good things to come. **God** is in the details of our lives from the very **beginning**. We see this in the patriarch Joseph's life (Gen 50:20). Ignatius does not want their *charitable love* misdirected to get him released and thus **spare** him, as it were, from **attaining to God** through his **lot** of martyrdom (Sal; for other passages on his **lot**, see Tr 12.3, Phld 5.1). There is no **attaining to God** without **obtaining grace**.

2

1. For I do not want you to be people pleasers, but to please God, just as you already do. As for me, I shall never again have such an opportunity to attain to God, and you, if you should happen to keep silent, shall never have a better deed inscribed. For if you should happen to keep silent and leave me alone, I shall become an intelligible word of God, but if instead you should happen to ardently love my flesh, I shall once again be just a vocal sound.

2. Grant me nothing more than to be poured out as a libation to God, while there is still an altar ready. That way you may form a chorus in love and sing to the Father in Jesus Christ that God has counted the bishop of Syria worthy of being found at the setting of the sun, after being summoned from whence it rises. It is a beautiful thing to be setting from the world poised toward God, that I may rise up to reach him.

IGNATIUS'S DESIRE TO BE A SACRIFICE

3

1. You have never beguiled anyone out of envy; you have taught others. Now, for my part, I want the instructions you give in making disciples to hold fast.

2

1. Ignatius wants them to **please God** by **keeping silent and leaving** him **alone**—instead of courting government officials to release him—so that he may **attain to God** through martyrdom and **become an intelligible word** to the pagans. Whether they **happen to** is up to them. Such **silence** will prove to be **a better deed** than they have thus far had **inscribed** in the Book of Life (Exod 32:33; Dan 12:1–3; Phil 4:3; Rev 3:5, 13:8, 17:8, 20:11–15, 21:27). Ignatius's **flesh** is his mere earthly, biological life, which possesses only the inarticulate and irrational **voice** of an animal.

2. The **libation** is Ignatius's blood; the **altar** is the arena in Rome (for Paul **being poured out as a libation**, a *drink offering*, see Phil 2:17, 2 Tim 4:6). The faithful **sing** as the accompanying **chorus** (cf. Eph 4.1–2). Only here does Ignatius call himself **bishop**. Why does he say **bishop of Syria**, rather than **of** Antioch? Perhaps he means *from* Syria, but elsewhere the same construction means **bishop of** (Mag 3.1, 15.1; Pol Sal). Or maybe **of Syria** means the same as **of** Antioch (but see comments on Eph 21.2). The simplest explanation is that Ignatius felt a personal responsibility to "*watch over*" (act as **bishop of**) all the faithful **of Syria** (cf. 9.1, Eph 21.2, Titus 1:5; on St. Polycarp over Asia, see Polycarp Intro, 157, fn. 1; Sm Sal; on St. Irenaeus over Gaul, see Ch Hist 5.23.4). Now **God** has **summoned** him **from Syria** in the east (where **the sun rises**) **to** Rome in the west (where **the sun sets**). Ignatius hopes thereby to die to this **world** and **rise up to reach God**.

IGNATIUS'S DESIRE TO BE A SACRIFICE

3

1. Ignatius knows they have **instructed others** to **hold fast** as **disciples** under persecution and torture, rather than **beguile** others to **envy** martyrs their lot. He wants them to do the same for him. He also is praising them for not **envying** his position as bishop, prospective martyr, and fellow **teacher**, and is humbly wishing them well **in making disciples** (5.3, 7.2; Mag 9.1; Eph 3.1, 1.2). Ignatius's posture of humble praise toward those who **envy** not, but aid those awaiting martyrdom, sets the tone for his coming appeals (in 3.2—9.1).

2. Just pray for me for strength, both inward and outward, that I may not only speak about it, but also want to do it, so that I may not only be called a Christian, but also prove to be one. For if I should prove to be one, I can also be called one, and then be found faithful whenever I am not seen in the world.

3. Nothing is good based on how it looks. In fact, it is by being in the Father that our God Jesus Christ is more clearly seen. Not the work of persuasive rhetoric, but rather feats of greatness characterize Christianity whenever it is hated by the world.

4

1. As for me, I am writing to all the churches and maintaining before everyone that I of my own free will am dying for God, unless you hinder me. I implore you: do not become "an untimely kindness" to me. Let me be the food of wild beasts; through them I can attain to God. I am God's wheat and am about to be ground fine by the teeth of wild beasts, that I may be found to be pure bread.

2. Better yet, coax the wild beasts to become my tomb and leave behind no trace of my body. That way I may burden no one when I fall asleep. When the world will not even see my body, then shall I truly be a disciple of Jesus Christ. Intercede with the Lord on my behalf that through these instruments I may prove to be a sacrifice to God.

2. When he says, **speak about it** and **want to do it**, Ignatius means his martyrdom. By this, he will make others **see** his acquisition of God's **strength** and clearly **prove** himself **to be a Christian** who has lived out his **faith** to "the end" (Eph 14.2). More literally, **seen** is *appear visible*, so the text can also be translated: **whenever I am not** *visible* **to the world**.

3. **How it looks** is, more literally, *its visible appearance* and **is more clearly seen** is *appears more visible*. While he was on earth **Jesus Christ** *appeared* to be only a man; in heaven, **in the Father's** bosom, he now *appears* **more clearly** to be **our God**. And he makes this **clear** to many **more** around **the world**, not to just a few in Judea (John 12:32, Matt 28:18–20, Acts 1:8). St. Ignatius's martyrdom will be a **great feat** that will "prove" that "actions speak louder than words" (3.2). The **greatness** of his martyrdom may even "make disciples" out of those in **the world** (3.1, Eph 10.1).

4

1. **Churches** probably refers to those along Ignatius's route, but perhaps to the congregations in Rome (Sal, 9.3). His allusion to Zenobius's adage, "**An untimely kindness** is no different than hostility" (Prov 1.20), sets up a paradox: his failure to die because of their **kind** appeal would be an **untimely** act of envy (9.2, 2.1, 5.3; see Acts 21:12–14 on Paul not wanting to be dissuaded). He wants his life to end as a sacrificial Eucharist, with his body as **God's wheat** becoming **pure bread** through his union with Christ's death (on both Ignatius and Polycarp being "a sacrifice," see 4.2, Mart Pol 14.2). St. Irenaeus quotes the last sentence in regard to the necessity of our trials (Ag Heresies 5.28.4).

2. **Better yet** contrasts with the "untimely kindness" (4.1) they must avoid. **Coax the wild beasts** is a dramatic way to say, *Beseech* **the Lord**. **Trace** is *a remnant* of his **body**, his *remains*, which we call *relics* (Mart Pol 17.1). Ignatius is mocking the Romans for whom the ultimate degradation was to have **no** body to bury or cremate. **To fall asleep** means to *die* (John 11:11–14, Acts 7:60, 1 Thess 4:13–18). **These instruments** are the teeth of **the wild beasts**. **To be a disciple of Jesus Christ** one must be **a sacrifice** pleasing **to God** (Rom 12:1; Eph 21.1; Phld 10.1; Mart Pol 1.1–2, 2.1, 4.1).

3. I am not giving you orders like Peter and Paul. They were apostles; I am a convict. They are free, while up until now I am a slave. But if I should suffer martyrdom, I shall become a freedman of Jesus Christ and rise up free in him. In the meantime, I am learning as a man in chains to long for nothing.

5

1. From Syria all the way to Rome I am fighting wild beasts, on land and sea, by night and day, chained to ten leopards (that is, to a detachment of soldiers), who only get worse the better they are treated. But I am becoming more of a disciple by their wrongs, "although not by this am I justified."

2. May I draw joy from the wild beasts prepared for me. I even wish they would make short work of me. Indeed I will coax them to devour me at once, unlike what they have done with some, whom they timidly held back from touching. And even if they be unwilling and refuse, I shall force them myself.

3. Grant me this concession: I know what is to my advantage. Now is the time I am beginning to be a disciple. May nothing seen or unseen keep me through envy from attaining to Jesus Christ. Come upon me fire and cross, packs of wild beasts, mutilations, rendings, wrenching of my bones, hacking of my limbs to pieces, repeated grinding of my whole body, cruel tortures of the devil—only let me attain to Jesus Christ!

3. Seeing himself far below **Peter and Paul**, Ignatius **gives** no **orders** (Tr 3.3). He hopes that his martyrdom will **free** him just as **Peter and Paul's** had **freed** them. **Suffer** and *passion* have the same root in Greek. Thus, by **suffering martyrdom**, Ignatius will be enduring his own *passion*. When circumstances around us control our ability to get what we **long for**, we must **learn** self-control and *crave* **nothing**.

5

1. What we have throughout this chapter may sound a bit melodramatic, but we cannot really imagine how it was for the saint. While facing his impending death, he is undergoing constant attack by **wild, beastly** men (Eph 1.2, 10.2; Rom 5.2; Dem 61). At their hands he is enduring **wrongs**, like our Lord did (Matt 27:27–31), and through this he is **becoming more of a disciple**. Nevertheless, "**not by this**" does he hope to be "**justified**" (1 Cor 4:4), but by the Lord's aiding his **disciple** to attain to God through his imminent and final **fight** in **Rome** (4.2, Phld 8.2, 1 Cor 4:4–5).

2. At times one or more of **the wild beasts** would **hold back** from attacking in the arena. Such **timidity** (or *cowardice*) in **the wild beasts** compares to the "*cowardice*" of Quintus in the arena, but contrasts with the valor of Germanicus that "turned *cowardice* into courage" (Mart Pol 4.1, 3.1). Whether by **coaxing** or by **force**, Ignatius will not be cheated. He is intent on becoming a disciple through his martyrdom and hopes to find **joy** in his own death, just as Jesus "endured the cross for the **joy** that was set before him" (Heb 12:2).

3. Ignatius is **beginning to be a disciple** because his **time** is at hand. The unseen who envy are **the devil** and his minions (Tr 4.2, 9.1). The **seen** are the ones who may unwittingly help **the devil** get him released (2.1—3.1). The Roman emperor Nero had nailed Christians to **crosses** and set them on **fire** to light up the games at night. The saint is prepared to endure all kinds of **tortures**, provided he **attains to Jesus Christ**.

6

1. Neither the delights of the world, nor the kingdoms of this age shall profit me at all. Dying to unite with Christ Jesus is better for me than reigning over the ends of the earth. Him I seek who died on our behalf. Him I want who rose for our sakes. The pangs of birth are upon me!

2. Indulge me, brothers and sisters. Do not get in the way of my living, nor want my dying. Do not favor the world by giving it the one who wants to be God's, nor entice him with the material things of earth. Let me receive pure light. Once I am there, I shall be a human being.

3. Let me be an imitator of the suffering of my God. If anyone has him within himself, let him understand what I long for and sympathize with me, knowing what urges me on.

IGNATIUS'S PASSION TO BE UNITED
WITH CHRIST'S PASSION

7

1. The ruler of this age wishes to snatch me away and corrupt my intention toward God. Therefore, none of you who are present are to assist him. Instead, be on my side, that is, on God's. Do not speak of Jesus Christ, while longing for the world.

6

1. Rome is **the ends of the earth** for Ignatius. He rejects all **the world's** temptations, including dominating others, just as **Christ** had before him (Matt 4:8–10). **Dying to unite with** can also be translated **dying** *for* or *to reach*. Our redemption comes from **Christ's** sinless **dying** and victorious **rising**. Ignatius compares his own martyrdom to giving **birth**. His **birth pangs** will be those of a newborn as it is pressed through **the birth** canal. Such will be his **birth pangs** as a martyr as this **world** pushes him out and he comes forth alive into heaven (Tr 11.2; Mart Pol 18.3, 19.2).

2. If the Roman Christians interfere with his martyrdom, they may hinder him from true **living** and **give him** to **the world**. Moreover, they may **entice him** to trade his heavenly birthright of **pure light** for an **earthly** morsel of no value (Heb 12:16–17; see 7.2 on Ignatius's loss "of love for **material things**"). To **receive pure light** is to receive Christ, for Christ is **light** (Eph 19.2), just as to become "**pure** bread" (Rom 4.1) is to become one with "the Living Bread" (John 6:51). **Human being** (or *man*) refers to "the new *man*" in Christ that we are to keep "putting on" in this life (Eph 4:24, Col 3:9–10, Gal 3:27, Eph 20.1, Mag 1.2), so that each of us may in the next life become completely **human** like Christ, who is the archetypal **human** (1 John 3:2; Sm 4.2; 1 Cor 15:21–22, 45–49; Phil 5.1; Ag Heresies 3.22.3).

3. To **imitate the** *passion* Ignatius must **suffer** and die as Christ **God** did. Full **understanding** comes from full union with **God**. Ignatius's "intention" to "be human" by "*reaching* Jesus Christ" (7.1, 6.2, 6.1) is **urgent**.

IGNATIUS'S PASSION TO BE UNITED WITH CHRIST'S PASSION

7

1. The Roman Christians might think they would be helping Ignatius by gaining his release, but unwittingly they would be taking the **side** of **the ruler of this age** and opposing Ignatius, who is on **God's side**. When we **long** (or *pine*) **for the world**, the devil gets what he **wishes** for.

2. Do not let beguiling envy dwell among you. And if, upon arriving, I should appeal to you myself, do not be persuaded by me. Instead, believe what I am writing to you. For though I am still alive, I am writing to you as one passionately desiring to die. My passionate desire has been crucified, and there is in me no fire of love burning for material things. Rather there is water living and speaking in me, saying to me from within, "Come to the Father."

3. I take no pleasure in corruptible food or in the pleasures of this life. I want the bread of God, which is the flesh of Christ, who is from the seed of David. And for drink I want his blood, which is incorruptible love.

8

1. I no longer want to go on living the way people typically do, and this shall be the case, if you should want it. So want it, that you also may be wanted.

2. With these few lines, I petition you: believe me. And in turn, Jesus Christ will make it clear to you that I am telling the truth. He is the never-lying mouth by which the Father has spoken truly.

3. Offer your petition for me that I may attain. I do not write you in keeping with what the flesh wants, but in keeping with what God intends. If I should happen to suffer martyrdom, it will be because you wanted it. If it turns out that I am rejected, it will be because you hated me.

2. **Envy** is the devil's destructive way (5.3, Tr 4.2). **Passionately desiring to die** refers to Ignatius's martyric death. **My passionate desire has been crucified** can refer to Jesus Christ and to Ignatius's former carnal **passions,** for in Christ his "flesh" **has been "crucified"** and he **has been "crucified** "to the world" (Gal 5:24, 6:14, 2:20; Mart Pol 22.1). **Passionate desire** (*eros*) is the love that yearns for union with one's beloved. Im**passioned desire** for Christ can redirect all **passions** falsely focused on the ego. Ignatius's **burning for material things** has been quenched by the **living water** of baptism welling up **from within** by the Spirit (John 4:10, 14; 7:37–39). Thus is the saint drawn **to the Father.**

3. Ignatius finds **no pleasure in** the **corruptible** things **of this life** (8.1, 7.2; Eph 9.2; Tr 6.2). Instead, he **wants** someone more substantial, **Christ,** the offspring *of David* (Eph 18.2, 20.2; Tr 9.1; Sm 1.1; 2 Tim 2:8). In this life we partake of **Christ's flesh and blood** in the Eucharist (John 6:47–58); in the next age we shall ever **drink** of **his incorruptible love. Love** could mean *love feast* (Sm 8.2), with Ignatius having in mind the eternal *love feast* which we shall enjoy in our **incorruptible** bodies (1 Cor 15:52–54, Rev 19:6–9).

8

1. He **no longer wants** (or *desires*) **to go on living** the way others **do** (Tr. 2.1). By **wanting** his martyrdom, the Roman Christians **may also be wanted** by Christ.

2. Here begins Ignatius's closing. Once they **believe** he "wants" martyrdom (8.1), they will "offer" their "**petition for**" him that he "may attain" to God (8.3 below).

3. Ignatius's request for prayer so that he may **attain to God** through **martyrdom** does not line up with the desires of **the flesh** (whether *carnal* or merely *physical*; cf. Luke 21:36). **But** his **petition is in keeping with God's intention** for his death and life. His future is in their hands, as it were. He will **suffer martyrdom if** they **want** that, or his own **petition to attain to God** will be **rejected if** they **petition** men for his release (1.2, 2.1–2, 4.1, 6.2–3, 7.1, 8.1–2).

FINAL REMARKS AND FAREWELL

9

1. Remember in your prayer the Church that is in Syria, which has God for its pastor instead of me. Jesus Christ alone will watch over it—along with your love.

2. But as for me, I am ashamed to be called one of them, for I am not worthy, since I am the least of them and one untimely born. But I have been granted mercy to be somebody—if it turns out that I attain to God.

3. My very spirit embraces you, as does the love of the churches. They welcomed me in the name of Jesus Christ, instead of treating me as a temporary visitor. As a matter of fact, those churches that did not lie along my planned route went before me from city to city.

10

1. Now I write these things to you from Smyrna through the Ephesians, who are most worthy of blessing. And also with me, along with many others, is Crocus, whose name is very dear to me.

2. Regarding those who have preceded me from Syria to Rome for the glory of God, I believe you have firsthand knowledge. Let them know that I am near, for they are all worthy of God and of you. It is right for you to refresh them in every way.

FINAL REMARKS AND FAREWELL

9

1. Although Ignatius has left, **the Church** throughout **Syria** is still in good hands. **God** himself is **its pastor** and **Christ will watch over it** (*be its bishop*; Rom 2.2, Pol Sal). Through **prayer**, the **love** of the Roman Christians **will** help tend the flock **in Syria**.

2. Ignatius humbly states that he is **not worthy** to be called a Christian from "Syria" (9.1, Sm 11.1). Like St. Paul, he speaks of himself as "**one** who was **untimely born**" (1 Cor 15:8–9), that is, *a miscarried fetus*, which could only be of use by God's grace. The successful outcome of **mercy granted** is **God attained**.

3. Even though Ignatius actually was **a temporary visitor, the churches** warmly **welcomed** him as a victor. Here we see his triumphant procession winding its *way* (**route**) **from city to city**, with representatives of **the churches going before** him on his *way* to Rome as a coming conqueror of death and the devil (Eph 9.2). Literally, **planned** is *according to the flesh*.

10

1. Ignatius wants the Roman Christians to know he is at **Smyrna** and that they should expect **Crocus** to carry his epistle to them once it reaches **Ephesus**. (For details on **Crocus's** "worthiness," see Eph 2.1.)

2. **Those who have preceded** him may have included Zosimus and Rufus, mentioned in connection with Ignatius by Polycarp (Phil 9.1). Even though Ignatius is in chains and "in peril" (Eph 12.1), he is thinking about how these men should be offered **refreshing** hospitality. By **near** St. Ignatius means he expects to be **near Rome** at the time his epistle is read to the faithful.

3. I am writing these things to you on the ninth day before the kalends of September. May you fare well all the way to the end in the patient endurance of Jesus Christ.

3. With the date of *August 24* (**the ninth day before the kalends of September** according to the Roman calendar) and with the date of Crocus's arrival (possibly by sea), the Roman Church should be able to estimate when Ignatius will arrive and so be ready to welcome him. But the date that really matters is **the end,** and up until then what matters is that we **fare well in the patient endurance of Jesus Christ** (Rev 1:9). This is exactly what Ignatius did. At the command of Trajan, the Roman emperor, he was fed to the lions in the arena at Rome and thereby attained to God as a perfect disciple of **Jesus Christ** (for details, see Ignatius Intro, 5–6). The Orthodox Church commemorates his life and martyrdom every year on December 20, the date found in *The Martyrdom* (7) and included in the *Synaxarion.*

The Epistle of St. Ignatius to the Philadelphians

CONTENTS

SALUTATION

Ignatius the God-bearer to the church of God the Father and the Lord Jesus Christ that is gathered at Philadelphia in Asia. You have been granted mercy and are firmly established in divine harmony. You are also rejoicing in the passion of our Lord without wavering and are fully convinced of his resurrection by experiencing his utter mercy. I embrace you in the blood of Jesus Christ as a church that is an eternal and constant joy. This is particularly so whenever you are at one with the bishop and with the presbyters and deacons who with him have been appointed as Jesus Christ intended. These he established authoritatively according to his own will by his Holy Spirit.

PRAISE FOR THEIR BISHOP

1

1. As for your bishop, I know that it was not from himself nor through human agency that he obtained the ministry that is for the common good of the community. And it was not because of vainglory either, but rather in the love of God the Father and the Lord Jesus Christ. I am struck by his forbearance. He can accomplish more when silent than those who talk on and on.

SALUTATION

Philadelphia was a wealthy hub for trade northeast of Tralles in the province of **Asia**. St. John wrote to its **church** (Rev 3:7–13). God's gifts to them include **divine harmony** (*one and the same godly mind*), **unwavering joy,** and **utter mercy**. These remain theirs as they **experience the Lord's passion** and **resurrection** (Mag 11.1, Sm 1.1, Mart Pol 19.1). Even so, Ignatius is concerned with a threat of "division" where some members might come to **be at** odds with **the bishop and** his clergy by following the "divisive" Judaizers, instead of **being at one** with their leaders and the Lord (2.1–2, 3.1–2, 6.1–3, 7.1–2, 8.1–2). **Appointed as intended** may point to their leaders being ordained by the apostles or their successors. **Established authoritatively** may indicate the same, as well as the manifestation of charismatic gifts (see Phld 7.2, Pol 2.2, 2 Tim 1:6, Mark 16:17–18, Heb 2:3–4). Instead of wishing them "abundant greetings" (cf. other Salutations), Ignatius proceeds to pressing leadership concerns (see 1.1).

PRAISE FOR THEIR BISHOP

1

1. Ignatius had met their **bishop** and had to **know** his name, as well as the names of the Judaizing leaders he withstood (6.3—8.2). But he does not tell us what they are. He will also refuse to name his opponents in Smyrna, hoping that they may "turn back." (Sm 5.3). "The name" that matters for Ignatius is **"Jesus Christ"** (6.1, 8.2, 10.1). His chief concern for the Judaizers is for them to "repent" and "rejoin" themselves "to the unity of God and the council of the **bishop**," and so be freed "from bondage" (8.1). Rather than giving their names, he just gives us their character. One Judaizer may have taken **ministry** upon **himself**. Perhaps another got other people to support him (cf. 1 Cor 1:10–12). Worst of all was leadership based on naked **vainglory**. But their **bishop** is different. His **ministry** is for **the common good,** not his own ego. Born out of **God's love,** it reflects the **forbearance** and **silence** that **Christ** showed at his passion in the face of those who went **on and on** *speaking* against him (Matt 26:66–68, 27:12–14; Eph 6.1, 15.1).

2. For he is attuned to the commandments as a lyre is to its strings. Therefore, my soul blesses his mindset toward God, recognizing it to be virtuous and perfect. It also blesses his unshakeable character, as well as his freedom from anger in all the forbearance of the living God.

EXHORTATION TO UNITY

2

1. Therefore, as children of the light of truth, flee division and evil teaching. And where the shepherd is, there you should follow like sheep.

2. For many wolves that come across as trustworthy use evil pleasure to try to take God's runners captive, but in your unity there will be no room for them.

3

1. Stay away from evil plants, which Jesus Christ does not cultivate, because they are not the Father's planting—not that I have found division among you, but rather a filtering out.

2. **The forbearance** (or *gentleness*) **of the living God** can also be translated *as one living in all godly forbearance*. **Forbearance** leads to **unshakeability** (see Heb 12:26–28 on **God shaking** heaven and earth) and also **freedom from anger**. Such dispassion is manifest when our temper is **free from** the domination of the passions (see Misc 2.13.59.6 on passion as misused appetite), under the Spirit's control, and **attuned to God's commandments** (see Eph 4.1 for the "council of presbyters" being "**attuned to** the bishop")."

EXHORTATION TO UNITY

2

1. Christians are **children of the light** that is **true** and the **truth** that enlightens. **Light** fills and unites, while **division** separates. **Truth** opposes **evil teaching**. Both Christ and his bishop are the **shepherd** (*pastor*) of the flock and both embody **light** and **truth**.

2. The **many wolves that** look **trustworthy** have **come** with "evil teaching" to "divide the sheep" (2.1, Matt 7:15, Acts 20:28–30). Such "teaching" may involve the **pleasures** of pride, which puff up and "divide" (3.3, 6.1–3, 7.2, 8.2; Tr 7.1; 2 Tim 3:1–8). If we would **unite** in "following the Shepherd" and his "shepherd," then these **wolves** would have **no room to** maneuver so as to "divide" (2.1) and **capture** us. So let us "**run**" together as **runners** who "**run** to win" (1 Cor 9:24; Eph 3.1—4.1; Pol 1.2, 6.1; Phil 9.2).

3

1. There is **no division among** this church's members. Rather, they are experiencing **a filtering out** (a *purifying*; Rom Sal). They are staying, even as those who are **dividing** off from them have gone **out** to schismatic groups, called **evil plants** (3.3; Tr 6.1—7.2, 11.1–2; Eph 10.3; 1 John 2:19; Ag Heresies 4.26.2). Observe the progression in 2.1—3.1: "**evil** teaching" leads to "evil pleasure," and these produce **evil plants**. In this epistle, **evil plants** are the various communities of the Judaizers. These heretical groups are many, but **the Father's planting** is one (1.1, 4.1; Matt 15:13).

2. For as many as belong to God and Jesus Christ, these are with the bishop. And as many as repent and come back to the unity of the church, these too will belong to God, so that they may live their lives in line with Jesus Christ.

3. Do not be deceived, my brothers and sisters. If anyone follows a schismatic, he is not going to inherit the kingdom of God. If anyone walks with an alien mindset, this person is not conforming to the passion.

4

1. Therefore, be eager to avail yourselves of one Eucharist, so that whatever you do, you may do it God's way. For there is one flesh of our Lord Jesus Christ, and one cup that brings union through his blood. And there is one altar, just as there is one bishop, together with the council of presbyters and the deacons, my fellow slaves.

2. **God and Jesus Christ** stay with all who stay **with the bishop**. If anyone **repents** from dividing himself off from **the bishop and comes back to the unity of the church, God will** receive him, because this is **in line with** "the intention of **Jesus Christ**," that we **live** our **lives in unity** (Sal, 2.1—3.3, 8.1). **Church unity** is a gift from **God** and **Christ** (Sal, 4.1, 5.2, 8.1, 9.1; Tr 11.2; Sm 12.2; Pol 1.2; Eph 4:3–6).

3. **Schismatics** are those who instigate or in some other way become part of a **schism** (a *splitting off*). **Schisms** involve "evil plants" (3.1) and come from **a mindset** that is **alien to** (or *estranged from*) **the passion** of Jesus Christ (6.2). **Schismatics** would rather exalt themselves than **conform to** his—and *agree to* suffer their own—**passion** (see Sm 5.1–3 regarding the Docetists).

4

1. While Ignatius could also be thinking of the Docetists when he mentions the **flesh of our Lord Jesus Christ** (5.1, Sm 7.1), the "schismatics" (3.3) he primarily has in mind are the Judaizers, though some of them could be Docetists as well. They are—and may be tempting others to be—performing separate **Eucharists**, probably on the Sabbath, apparently in several separate communities in the vicinity of Philadelphia (1.1, 3.1, 6.1–2, 7.2, 8.1–2, 9.1–2; cf. Mag 9.1). They promote a separate **cup** from the **one cup that brings union** (or *unity*) **through his blood**. The proper **way** is **God's way**, the **one way** of **union** (Mag 7.1–2). We should **be eager** for that.

THE APOSTLES AND PROPHETS PREACHED JESUS CHRIST, NOT JUDAISM

5

1. My brothers and sisters, I am overflowing with love for you, and with joy beyond measure I am watching out for your safety—yet not I, but Jesus Christ. As a criminal in chains for him, I am all the more fearful, since I am still imperfect. But as your prayer reaches God, it will bring me to perfection in my obtaining the lot by which I have been shown mercy. This will happen by my fleeing for refuge to the gospel as to the flesh of Jesus and to the apostles as to the Church's council of presbyters.

2. And the prophets we love as well, because they too directed their proclamation toward the gospel, both hoping for him and waiting for him. By putting their faith in him they also obtained salvation, since they were in the unity of Jesus Christ. As saints they are worthy of love and admiration, being approved by Jesus Christ and numbered together with us in the gospel of the common hope.

THE APOSTLES AND PROPHETS PREACHED
JESUS CHRIST, NOT JUDAISM

5

1. Ignatius hopes his **love for** them will become an **overflowing** "libation" (Rom 2.2), but he **fears** lest his **criminal** status not be **perfected** by his martyrdom. Jesus himself was **perfected** by his own sacrificial death (Luke 13:32; Heb 2:10, 5:8–9; Phil 2:8–11). Even so, Ignatius is confident that their **prayer will perfect** him, that is, enable him to **obtain** his **lot** of martyrdom. In a broader sense, **the lot** may include Ignatius's lifelong embracing of the cross, **by which he has** already received **mercy**. He is preparing himself for martyrdom **by fleeing for refuge**. The gospel is *the good news* of salvation through **Christ's** death and resurrection. "**The flesh of Jesus Christ** is the Eucharist" (Sm 7.1), the embodiment of our salvation and an exhortation to our own self-sacrifice. **The apostles** model a martyric faith in and love for **the gospel** message of salvation, and **as the Church's council of presbyters** they reign with **Christ** (see the *elders* in Rev 4–5).

2. Ignatius now makes clear that **the prophets** and **the gospel** go **together** (cf. 6.1–2, 8.2). **The unity** of the Church includes **the prophets because their proclamation** was **directed toward the gospel** (*the good news* of his victorious coming) and **they hoped for, awaited, and** *believed* **in him** (or *it*, that is, **the gospel**). **Christ** *bears* **approving** *witness to* their **saintliness** (*holiness*) **and numbers** them with the apostles (5.1) and the faithful within **the unity of Jesus Christ** (4.1, 5.1). Through **the gospel, the prophets** share in **common** with all **of us the hope of salvation** in **Christ**.

IGNATIUS EXALTS JESUS CHRIST OVER JUDAISM

6

1. But if anyone should expound Judaism to you, do not listen to him. For it is better to hear about Christianity from a man who is circumcised than about Judaism from a man who is uncircumcised. Moreover, if either of them should fail to speak of Jesus Christ, to me they are tombstones and graves of the dead, upon which only men's names are inscribed.

2. Flee, then, the base tricks and traps of the ruler of this age, that you may avoid his oppressive intention and not grow weak in love. Instead, let everyone join in the common assembly with an undivided heart.

3. Now I thank my God that I have a clear conscience in relation to you, and that nobody has a claim of which to boast, whether secretly or openly, that I burdened anyone in anything small or great. Moreover, my request is that all those among whom I spoke may not have this as a testimony against them.

7

1. For even though certain people desired to deceive me, in keeping with the flesh, yet the Spirit is not deceived, since he is from God. For he "knows from whence he comes and where he is headed," and he exposes what is hidden. I cried out while among you; I kept saying with a loud voice, the voice of God, "Give heed to the bishop, to the council of presbyters, and to the deacons."

IGNATIUS EXALTS JESUS CHRIST OVER JUDAISM

6

1. **Expound** can also be rendered *interpret*. Whenever Ignatius mentions Judaism, he may have in mind one or more of these varieties: a pre-Christian form of **Judaism**, a post-Christian form of **Judaism**, or a **Judaizing Christianity** that is mixing old Jewish elements with the gospel (for passages on Jews, **Judaism**, and **Judaizers**, see Mag 7.2—11.1 and Phld 2–9, and more particularly, Mag 8.1, 10.1–3; Phld 6.2, 7.2, 8.1–2; Sm 1.2; Mart Pol 2.1, 3.2, 12.2—13.1, 17.2, 18.1). The last group tends to exalt Jewish scripture and *interpretation* above **Jesus Christ** (5.2, 6.2, 8.2), so there is no reason to **listen to** it. **Either of them** refers to **circumcised** and **uncircumcised** men who do not properly honor the **name** of **Jesus Christ**. In St. John's letters to the seven churches, those in Philadelphia and Smyrna who falsely claim to be Jews are really "the synagogue of Satan" (Rev 3:7, 9; 2:8–9; Mart Pol 13.1).

2. **Traps** can be translated *snares*, *plots*, and *ambushes*. **Base tricks and traps** refer to Judaizing exegesis, which can *ensnare* its prey in pride (8.2). **The ruler of this age** *plots* to *ambush* and **divide** our **hearts** and our **assemblies** (cf. Eph 14.1, Tr 13.2). To **flee** this, we must each **join** together **in love** around the Eucharist (10.1, Eph 13.1).

3. There may be some people that have left who are **secretly** spreading lies about Ignatius, but he has **burdened nobody**. Instead, his *wish* **is that any claim** like **this** will not become **a testimony against** those who would **boast** "deceitfully" (7.1).

7

1. **In keeping with the flesh** may refer to our fallen humanity with its *carnal* orientation that opposes **the Spirit** (7.2), or to our acting *in a human way*, or to a combination of these. Unlike those who **desire to deceive, the Spirit** "knows from whence he comes and where he is headed" (John 3:8, 8:14–15). **Hidden** probably refers back to "secretly" in 6.3. Earlier, Ignatius had **cried out** in **the Spirit** before he **knew** that some had left the church with its **bishop** and clergy.

2. Now there were those who suspected me of saying these things because I knew in advance about the division caused by certain people. But he is my witness—for whom I am in chains—that I did not learn this from a human source. No, it was the Spirit who was doing the proclaiming, saying these utterances:

"Do nothing apart from the bishop."
"Keep your flesh as the temple of God."
"Love union."
"Flee from divisions."
"Become imitators of Jesus Christ,
even as he is of his Father."

8

1. As for me, then, I was doing my part as a man ready for union; but where there is division and anger, God does not dwell. Consequently, the Lord forgives all who repent, provided it turns out that their repentance rejoins them to the unity of God and the council of the bishop. I have faith in the grace of Jesus Christ, who will release you from everything that holds you in bondage.

2. Moreover, I exhort you to do nothing that promotes cliquish ambition, but to act in accordance with learning Christ. For I heard certain people saying, "Unless I find it in the archives, I do not believe it in the gospel." And when I said to them, "It is written," they answered me, "That is the question that lies before us." But to me the archives are Jesus Christ. The inviolable archives are his cross and death and his resurrection and the faith that comes through him. It is by these, through your prayer, that I want to be justified.

2. **Union** with God and *unity* in the church are both one, while heretical **divisions** are many (1.1, 3.1, 8.1). When Ignatius refers to **the division** (or *separation*) caused **by certain people**, he is speaking about the "schism" "planted" by the Judaizers (see 3.3, 3.1; Mag 4.1). When he exhorts them to **flee from divisions** (cf. Sm 7.2), he is telling them to *run away* **from** the **divisions** associated with heretical offshoots (Tr 11.1). This would include any **divided** relationships and **divisiveness** of heart that would *separate* them from **God** (Eph 14.1, Tr 13.2, Phld 6.2). **Certain** Judaizers prided themselves on knowing better than the leaders of the church in Philadelphia (8.2, 1.1). Ignatius contrasts two ways of knowing: from **a human source** (literally, **human** *flesh*—whether carnally disposed or not) and from **the Spirit** (7.1, Eph 8.2). His prophetic **utterances** insightfully addressed the temptations that had led **certain people**—and could also lead others—to schism: acting **apart from the bishop**; desecrating our God-given **flesh**; putting self ahead of **union** (or *unity*) with **God** and others; entertaining **divisive** groups, actions, and attitudes; and preferring anything else to **imitating Jesus Christ as he imitates his Father.**

8

1. **The bishop** has his **part** in promoting **union**, but it is up to the **angry** and **divisive** to **repent and** enter back into **God's unity.** They have lost the Christian way of life as a sharing in **God's** gift of **unity: union** with **God, Jesus Christ,** our ministers, and each other (cf. 9.1). **The Lord** wants a **repentance** that **reunites** us with our leaders, so he may **forgive** us and **release** (or *loose*) us **from every** sin that **binds** (cf. Eph 19.3, Matt 16:19, Pol 5.2), such as "cliquish ambition" (8.2).

2. The Judaizers's **cliquish ambition** demanded finding in the Old Testament (**the archives lying** open **before** them in some of its books) everything contained **in the gospel** (perhaps as **found in** a copy of *Matthew's Gospel lying* open *in front of* them). **Jesus Christ** is the preexistent Word **written in** the scriptures that his disciples need to **learn** and **the** new glorified **archives (the** *depository*) in whom **faith** and **the faith** are **found** (Rom 7:6). His Passover from **death** to **resurrection** life is **the inviolable** lens through which Christians see the Old Testament (9.1–2, Luke 24:44–48). Over all this the Judaizers and Docetists stumbled. Here **to be justified** is to attain to God (cf. Rom 5.1).

9

1. The priests, too, were good, but better yet the High Priest entrusted with the holy of holies. He alone has been entrusted with the secrets of God, since he himself is the Father's door, through which enter Abraham and Isaac and Jacob and the prophets and the apostles and the Church, all these, into the unity of God.

2. But the gospel has something so special: the coming of the Savior, our Lord Jesus Christ, his passion, and the resurrection. For the beloved prophets pointed to him in their proclamation, but the gospel is the finished work of incorruptibility. All these things, taken together, are beautiful, provided you believe with love.

SENDING AN ENVOY TO THE CHURCH AT ANTIOCH

10

1. Since it has been reported to me that the church at Antioch in Syria is at peace, in keeping with your prayer and the compassion you have in Christ Jesus, it is right for you as a church of God to appoint a deacon to travel there as God's envoy. That way, when they have joined in the common assembly, you can congratulate them and glorify the name.

9

1. Jewish **priests** are good, but cannot be compared to our **High Priest**, Jesus Christ (Heb 4:14—10:25). Entrusted with **God's secret** mysteries (Rev 3:7), and the meaning of the Old Testament (8.2–9.2), **he is the door** (John 10:7, 9) **through which** the godly of all time **enter into unity** (8.1, Sm 12.2, Pol 8.3, Tr 11.2).

2. **The gospel** is superior to the Old Testament. It is the *good news* that **our Savior Jesus** the **Christ** has **come** with his new covenant (for more on the *newness* of **his coming**, see Eph 19.2–3, Ag Heresies 4.34.1–3). By **his passion and resurrection**, Jesus has ushered in the **incorruptibility the prophets** had foreseen (especially David in Ps 15/16:10; Acts 2:25–32, 13:35–37). **The prophets** and **the gospel** together bring us **beauty**, not rancor, **provided** we do not divide the faith from **love**.

SENDING AN ENVOY TO THE CHURCH AT ANTIOCH

10

1. The **peace** that came to **Antioch** was once seen as the cessation of persecution there (cf. Mart Ign 1–2), which may have ended after Trajan left for the East. Polycarp's martyrdom brought "an end to persecution" in Smyrna (Mart Pol 1.1), so perhaps the condemnation of Ignatius helped do the same for **Antioch**. Current scholarship, however, thinks Ignatius's mention of **peace** refers to a division between Jewish and Gentile Christians that has yielded to unity (cf. 4.1, 8.1—9.2, 11.1; Sm 1.2, 11.2–3; Pol 7.1; Gal 2:1–21). **Joining in the common assembly** means gathering to celebrate the Eucharist (6.2; Eph 5.3, 13.1, 20.2; Mag 7.2). Hallmarks of such a gathering are **peace** and unity (Eph 13.1–2, Mag 6.2—7.2, Phld 4.1, Sm 12.2). **The name** is a Jewish way to speak about **God** that here may refer to **Christ** as **God** (10.2; Eph 1.1, 1.2, 3.1, 7.1; cf. Matt 28:19, where our Lord mentions **the name** when he speaks of the Trinity). Using the expression **the name** may help Ignatius connect with the Jewish Christians in **Antioch** and Philadelphia, as well as with the Judaizers.

2. Blessed in Jesus Christ is the man who will be counted worthy of such a ministry—and you too will be glorified. If you are willing, it is not impossible for you to do this for the name of God, since even the churches close by have sent bishops, and others have sent presbyters and deacons.

FINAL REMARKS AND FAREWELL

11

1. Now about Philo, the deacon from Cilicia: as a man well-attested, he is even now assisting me in the word of God alongside Rheus Agathopus, an elect man who is following me from Syria after leaving this life behind. They also bear you witness—and I myself thank God on your behalf—that you received them even as the Lord receives you. But may those who dishonored them be redeemed by the grace of Jesus Christ.

2. The love of the brothers and sisters in Troas embraces you. From there also I am writing you through Burrhus, who was sent along with me by the Ephesians and Smyrnaeans as a matter of honor. The Lord Jesus Christ will honor them, on whom they place their hope in body, soul, and spirit, with faith, love, and harmony. May you fare well in Christ Jesus, our common hope.

2. By **sending** an "envoy" as instructed, the **deacon** will be **blessed** and the church **will be glorified**—and so will **God's "name"** (10.1). Personal sacrifice for **God** is costly, but **if you are willing, it is not impossible for you.**

FINAL REMARKS AND FAREWELL

11

1. **Deacons Philo** and **Rheus Agathopus** have arrived from Antioch with news of "peace" (10.1, cf. Sm 10.1). Like them, let us be **well-attested** and **elect** servants who **have left behind** our **life** in **this** world (cf. Eph 9.2). And like the Philadelphians, may we **receive** others **as the Lord receives** us. As for **those who dishonor God's** leaders, like the Judaizers did these **deacons,** let us want **them** to find **redemption** in **Christ.**

2. Ignatius is writing this epistle and his last two—to the **Smyrnaeans** and St. Polycarp—from **Troas,** on the Asiatic coast, right across from Europe. **Burrhus** may be Ignatius's amanuensis (scribe) or the carrier of this epistle (for more on him, see Eph 2.1, Sm 12.1). As we are commanded to "love the Lord **with** all [our] heart and **soul** and mind and strength" (Mark 12:30), so the Philadelphians are to **place their hope on the Lord with** all their being and all their virtues. **Faith, love, and harmony** involve our relationship with **Christ** and others. By these virtues energizing us, **may** we become "entirely sanctified" and "be preserved blameless" in "**spirit, soul, and body** [Ignatius actually uses the word *flesh*]" "at our **Lord's** coming" (1 Thess 5:23).

The Epistle of St. Ignatius to the Smyrnaeans

CONTENTS

SALUTATION

Ignatius the God-bearer to the church of God the Father and the beloved
Jesus Christ that is gathered at Smyrna in Asia. You are mercifully gifted
with every grace and filled with faith and love—and you lack no spiritual
gift. You are most worthy of God and a bearer of the holy. Abundant greetings in a blameless spirit and the Word of God.

GLORIFYING CHRIST AND HIS TRUE CROSS

1

1. I glorify Jesus Christ, the God who made you so wise, for I am aware that
you are settled in an immovable faith, having been nailed, as it were, to the
cross of the Lord Jesus Christ in both flesh and spirit. And I recognize that
you are firmly established in love by the blood of Christ and fully convinced
by experience concerning our Lord that

> he is truly of the lineage of David
> according to the flesh,
> and Son of God
> according to God's will and power;
> truly born of a virgin,
> and baptized by John,
> that all righteousness might be fulfilled by him;

SALUTATION

Smyrna was a rich metropolis and port on the Mediterranean Sea. It lay northwest of Ephesus and vied with it for preeminence in the province of **Asia** (as this regards Polycarp, see Polycarp Intro, 157, fn. 1). It was from **Smyrna** that Ignatius sent his *Epistle to the Romans* (see comments on Rom 10.1). **Bearer of the holy** is similar to "God-bearers" and "bearers of holy things" (Eph 9.2). When capitalized, **Word of God** refers to *the Logos*, a title John used for **Christ** (John 1:1, 14; 1 John 1:1; Rev 19:13; also see Mag 8.2, 7.2; Phld 8.2; Eph 15.2; Ag Heresies 3.11.1; Dem 6). **Word of God** could mean scripture here, but whenever Ignatius mentions **blameless** and **abundant greetings** in other epistles (Eph Sal, Rom Sal), he is referring to **Christ**. **A blameless spirit** can also be rendered *the* **blameless** *Spirit* (for an example of Irenaeus linking together the work of **the Word** and *the Spirit*, see Ag Heresies 4.20.1).

GLORIFYING CHRIST AND HIS TRUE CROSS

1

1. **The cross** makes Christians **so wise** (1 Cor 1:17–25). The **faith** of the Smyrnaeans is **immovable** because they **have** allowed themselves to **be nailed** (sharply and painfully attached) **to the cross**. They endure this because they are **fully convinced that our Lord** is **truly flesh** and **truly Son of God**. This **full** conviction is theirs **by the experience** of being **fully established in love by the blood of Christ** that was once for all shed on **the cross** and is now received in the Eucharist (Mag 7.2, 11.1; Phld Sal). **In flesh and spirit** refers to the totality of their humanity. **Truly** means *in fact, really*, or *actually*. By repeating **truly** in this anthem (1.1b–2), Ignatius stresses that our **faith** in **Christ** rests on *actual* historical events, including his manifested **Son**ship (Rom 1:3–4) and his **virginal** birth and **baptism** (Matt 1:20–23, 3:13–15).

2. and truly under Pontius Pilate and Herod the Tetrarch
nailed for us in the flesh
(from the tree's fruit we are,
from his passion blessed by God),
that through the resurrection he might raise
a banner for the ages for his holy and faithful ones,
whether among Jews or among Gentiles,
in the one Body of his Church.

TRUE PASSION AND RESURRECTION, INSTEAD OF DOCETIC SEEMING

2

1. For he suffered all these things for our sakes, in order that we might be saved. Indeed, he truly suffered, just as he also truly raised himself. He did not, as certain unbelievers say, seem to suffer—rather they themselves are the ones doing the seeming! Indeed, just as they think, so shall it happen to them, when they become bodiless and like phantoms.

3

1. For I myself do know and believe that even after the resurrection he was in the flesh.

2. In fact, when he came to Peter and those about him, he said to them, "Take hold and handle me, and see that I am not a bodiless phantom." And immediately they touched him and believed, being mingled with his flesh and spirit. Therefore, they scorned even death, and were found to be beyond death.

2. Ignatius expressly opposes the Gnostic opinions of the Docetists when he says that we can be **nailed** for "Jesus Christ" (1.1) because he was **truly "nailed" for us** (Ps 118:120 LXX)—both at certain *actual* points **in his flesh** and at a specific point in time **under Pontius Pilate and Herod the Tetrarch** (Acts 4:26–27, Luke 23:6–12; **Herod** is also known as Antipas). **God** has **blessed the** cross on which he was **nailed** to become **the tree** of life (Tr 11.2). The **banner** is the military *standard* of **the** cross that our **resurrected** Lord **raises** before his army of **holy** (or *saints*) **and faithful ones** (Isa 5:26, 49:22, 62:10). Together **Jews** and **Gentiles** make up **the one Body of his Church** (Eph 2:11–22, Phld 10.1, Sm 11.2).

TRUE PASSION AND RESURRECTION, INSTEAD OF DOCETIC SEEMING

2

1. Ignatius uses the words translated **think** and **seem** for his opponents because the Greeks used them when speaking subjectively. He uses the objective word **truly** to make a strong contrast between his Docetist antagonists and Christ, who **truly suffered** and **truly raised himself**, which a **phantom** cannot do (in Tr 9.2, "the Father" is the one "**raising** him"). The Docetist **unbelievers** are the *faithless* who fake being Christians by **seeming** to be **thinkers** (cf. Tr 10.1). *In reality,* the **bodiless** spiritual resurrection they expect at death will only leave them united to *demons* (another meaning of the Greek for **phantom**) and outside "the one **Body** of his Church" (1.2).

3

1. **Knowing and believing** is a stronger and more definite way to refer to Christ **being in the flesh after the resurrection** than "seeming" and "thinking" (2.1).

2. Ignatius continues to contrast Christ, who is neither **bodiless** nor **a phantom** (or *demon*), with the Docetists. **Flesh and spirit** refer to Christ's glorified humanity (cf. 3.3, 12.2; Eph 7.2; Mag 1.2). If **spirit** is translated as *breath*, then **mingled** refers to the apostles coming in *close contact* **with his flesh and** *breath* (cf. Luke 24:36–43, John 20:19–29, Eph 17.1–2; for more on **mingled**, see Eph 5.1, Ag Heresies 5.6.1, Dem 97).

3. And after the resurrection, he ate and drank with them as a man of flesh, even while spiritually he was united to the Father.

4

1. Now I am warning you about these things, beloved ones, even though I know that you too have the same perspective. Furthermore, I am protecting you in advance from the wild beasts in human form. Not only must you not welcome them, but, if possible, do not even meet with them face to face. But only pray for them, that if somehow they might happen to repent, despite it being difficult. Nevertheless, Jesus Christ, our true life, has power over this.

2. For if these things seemed to be accomplished by our Lord, then I too seem to be in chains. Why, moreover, have I given myself up to death, to fire, to sword, to wild beasts? Despite appearances, near the sword is near to God and in the midst of wild beasts is in the midst of God. Only let it be in the name of Jesus Christ, that I may suffer together with him! I am patiently enduring all things, since the perfect man himself empowers me.

5

1. Certain people ignore and deny him—but what matters most, they have been denied by him, since they are advocates of death rather than of truth. Neither the prophecies nor the law of Moses have persuaded them; and, thus far, not even the gospel or our own individual sufferings.

3. Christ is just as much **flesh** as we are. He demonstrated this when **he ate and drank with** the apostles **after the resurrection** (Luke 24:40–43, John 21:1–15, Acts 10:40–41). But **he** was not in "demonic" *union with* his **Father**, as the Docetists were with theirs (2.1, 3.2; John 8:44)! Rather his *union* is **spiritual.**

4

1. In two other epistles Ignatius seeks to **protect** others **in advance** (Mag 11.1, Tr 8.1). Part of his preparation for encountering **the wild beasts** in Rome is his interaction with **wild beasts in human form**, his Roman guards (Rom 5.1–2) and the heretics (here and in Eph 7.1). Having split themselves off from the truth, the Docetists have become false evangelists and deadly foes who are consumed by death (Tr 11.1; Phld 3.3, 6.1; Sm 5.1–2). **Welcome** may also be translated *let in* (Eph 9.1, 2 John 10–11). It is only by **prayer** and the **power** of **Christ, our true life, that they might happen to repent.** Nothing is too **difficult** for him.

2. What **our Lord accomplished** were the mighty acts of salvation: his coming in the flesh, his *passion*, and his raising himself from the dead (1–3). Behold **the perfect man**, our **power** in **all things!** He is our **power** in *every* weakness, *every* attack of the evil one, *every* circumstance (Phil 4:13, 2 Cor 12:9–10). **God is near** when we are at the point of **the sword.** Whenever we are **in the midst of** any frightening danger, let us picture ourselves safely nestled in **God's** arms. **Knowing** we are in his bosom draws us to **suffer together with Christ**, to "share in his **sufferings**" as we **suffer** our own (Phil 3:8–10, Tr 13.3, Phil 9.2).

5

1. Lest we **deny him** and get **denied by him** (see **deny** in 5.2, Mag 9.1, 2 Pet 2:1, 2 Tim 2:12–13), let us never **ignore** (or *refuse to know*) **him.** Those who **ignore and deny him** go on to reject the fourfold witness of **prophecy, Mosaic law, gospel**, and the **individual sufferings** of Christians and the martyrs's *passions*. Instead, they **advocate** as lawyers in the court of popular "opinion" (5.2) where **truth** is absent and **death** holds sway.

2. As a matter of fact, they hold the same opinion about us. For how does it help me if somebody praises me but blasphemes my Lord by refusing to confess that he is a flesh-bearer? Now the one who does not acknowledge this denies him completely and is a corpse-bearer.

3. Now recording their names did not seem right to me, since they belong to unbelievers. Indeed, far be it from me to even remember them until they turn back to the passion, which is our resurrection.

CHRIST'S BLOOD, BODY, AND BISHOP, INSTEAD OF DOCETIC PRIDE

6

1. Let no one be deceived: even the powers of heaven, the glory of angels, and the principalities, both seen and unseen, if they should fail to believe in the blood of Christ, for them also judgment is coming. Let him accept it who can. Let position puff up no one, for faith and love are everything. Nothing is preferable to them.

2. **The opinion** of the Docetists **about** "our sufferings" (5.1) is **the same blasphemy** as their **opinion about** our **Lord's** passion in the **flesh**. Thus, the "advocates of death" (5.1) become pall**bearers**, carrying their spiritually dead **corpses** to their own funerals, while our risen **flesh-bearing Lord** lives and enlivens us!

3. **Turn back** is a translation of *metanoia*, the word usually rendered *repentance*, which means *a change of mind, direction, and actions*. Only when the Docetists **turn back** will Ignatius **remember their names** in prayer in the Eucharistic Liturgy (cf. Sm 7.2; Phld 6.1, 1.1). His **passion** and **resurrection**—and their outworking in **our** lives—are intertwined and inseparable. Pascha, his Passover from death to life, is one (see Mag 15.1 for comments on **which is**; see Phld 8.2 for comments on "His cross and death and resurrection"). And so the *Troparion Hymn of Pascha* (Easter) connects Christ's **passion** and **resurrection**:

> Christ is risen from the dead,
> Trampling down death by death,
> And upon those in the tombs
> Bestowing life!

CHRIST'S BLOOD, BODY, AND BISHOP, INSTEAD OF DOCETIC PRIDE

6

1. In every Divine Liturgy, the cherubim, the seraphim, and all **the** godly **powers of heaven** worship with the **faithful**, in contrast to the evil cosmic **powers** extolled by the Gnostic Docetists (compare **the glory of angels**—or *glorious position of angels*—with "the positions assigned to **angels**" in Tr 5.2 and "the Aeons" in Eph 19.2). By their participation in the Divine Liturgy, they show that **they believe in the blood of Christ** offered for all in his passion and offered to the **faithful** in the cup of salvation. **If** these exalted **powers prefer faith and love** to being **puffed up**, how much more should one who holds a **position** in a church, for **judgment is coming** (on a **puffed-up** presbyter, see 8.1–2, 9.1).

2. But carefully note those who follow heterodox approaches to the grace of Jesus Christ that has come to us—how they are opposed to God's mindset. For love they have no regard: none for the widow, none for the orphan, none for the distressed, none for the prisoner in chains or the one released, and none for the hungry or thirsty.

7

1. They avoid Eucharist and prayer because they refuse to acknowledge that the Eucharist is the flesh of our Savior Jesus Christ, the flesh that suffered for our sins, which the Father in his kindness raised up. Those, then, who speak against God's bountiful gift are dying even while disputing. But it would be more to their advantage to show love, that they might also rise up.

2. It is right, then, to avoid such people, and to not even speak about them, either privately or publicly. Do give heed, however, to the prophets, and especially to the gospel. In it, the passion is made clear to us and the resurrection is accomplished. But flee their divisions as the beginning of evils.

2. The root for **heterodox** means *another of a different kind* (for more on **heterodoxy** and orthodoxy, see Mag 8.1, 11.1). Orthodoxy (right opinion and right glorifying) and orthopraxy (right practice) belong together. Otherwise, some kind of **heterodox approach** (with *different opinions* and *different glorifying*) that is deficient in **grace** and **love** will slip in. When people are deprived of **the grace of Jesus Christ**, who is "the **mindset** of the Father" (Eph 3.2), all that is left are *different opinions*. The Church at Rome is a "preeminent" example of **love** (*agape*) for others on account of its "*charity*" (*agape*; Rom Sal, 1.2; cf. Matt 25:31–46, Phil 6.1). This is just the sort of **love** the Docetists lack, since they lack "the **God**" who "is **Love**" (1 John 4:8, Tr 5.2). **Love** may include *a love feast* (8.2), a weekly community meal used to feed **the hungry**.

7

1. Those "following heterodox approaches" in 6.2 are the Docetists, who will not join in the **Eucharist** of the faithful **because they refuse to** believe that it is **the flesh of Christ**, his true body, *which* truly **suffered for our sins**. Since, for them, Jesus Christ only seemed to have a body, the Eucharist could only seem to be his body and blood. (For Irenaeus's remarks on Gnostic inconsistencies in offering a Eucharist, see Ag Heresies 4.18.4–5.) **Suffered** can also be rendered *endured the passion* (cf. 4.2). They stubbornly **refuse** to **acknowledge** (or *confess*) because they **love** not, and they **love** not because they approach "the grace of **Jesus Christ**" in a "heterodox" way (6.2). The Docetists may also be influencing others to separate from the true common **prayer** and **Eucharist** of the church and instead "perform" other church activities "apart from the bishop", such as a "baptism or love feast" (8.1–8.2, 9.1; Tr 7.2).

2. Ignatius exhorts the Smyrnaeans to **avoid** the Docetists who "**avoid** Eucharist and [**public**] prayer" (7.1) and to "**flee their**" schismatic "**divisions**" (Phld 7.2; see comments on Phld Sal, 1.1), because these will lead to all manner **of evils**. They are, **however**, to *listen to and carefully obey* **the gospel**, which **clearly** sets forth **the passion and the resurrection**.

8

1. You must all follow the bishop, as Jesus Christ does the Father. Follow, too, the council of presbyters as you do the apostles, and show reverence for the deacons as you do for what God commands. Let no one perform anything involving the church without the bishop. Regard that Eucharist as authorized which is celebrated under the oversight of the bishop or by whomsoever he himself permits.

2. Wherever the bishop appears, there let the entire community be present; just as wherever Jesus Christ is, there is the Catholic Church. It is not permitted either to baptize or to hold a love feast apart from the bishop. But whatever he does approve, this indeed is well-pleasing to God, that everything you do may be safe and authorized.

9

1. Furthermore, it is sensible for us to recover our sobriety while the time is still favorable for repenting and returning to God. It is good to recognize God and the bishop. The one who honors the bishop is honored by God. The one who performs any service secretly without the bishop is worshiping the devil.

8

1. **Following Bishop** Polycarp is the best way to "flee" heterodox "divisions" (7.2; about these see 6.2—7.2). It seems that a "puffed-up" **presbyter** (6.1) had left for a Docetist sect and was—or had the intention of—**performing** some kind of separate **Eucharist** *without* **the bishop's permission.** To prevent this, Ignatius directs that **presbyters** be **followed** as members of a group **(the council of presbyters)** which is **under the bishop,** and not individually. Even today, when a **presbyter** does preside at the altar in the absence of **the bishop** (which was necessary when Ignatius left Antioch for his martyrdom), **the bishop's authorization** is required. A **presbyter** may only preside over a **Eucharist** where **the bishop's** signed antimension is on the altar and he has been duly assigned by **the bishop. Authorized** can also be translated *certain,* both here and in 8.2.

2. The word for **entire community** means *fullness* or *multitude* and can be translated *congregation.* Here it seems to contain both ideas. **Catholic** literally means *according to the whole* and pertains to that indivisible quality of **the Church** by which the fullness of **Christ** is *wholly* manifest in every **church.** This is the first instance of the term in Christian literature (for others, see Mart Pol Sal, 8.1, 16.2, 19.2, Mosc 22.2). **The Catholic Church** can refer to the *universal* **Church** or **the** local **church** as distinct from heretical sects, which act **apart from the bishop** (cf. Eph 6.2). The Orthodox believe that they are **the Catholic Church** confessed in the Nicene Creed. The **love feast** (*agape*) was a meal that used to be eaten in connection with the Eucharist (Jude 12, 1 Cor 11:20–34, Did 9–10, Rom 7.3, Sm 6.2).

9

1. **Repenting** is always the **sensible,** the *reasonable,* thing to do (cf. Mag 7.1). We should do it now, **while** *we* **still** *have* **time,** thus abandoning the stupor of insubordinate sin (8.1–2) for **sobriety** (*clear-headedness;* Pol 2.3). **Favorable time** is *kairos* (for more on **time,** see Pol 3.2). We should never presume that there will be another *opportunity* **(favorable time)** to **repent.** To **recognize God and the bishop** is to see them for who they are and treat them accordingly. **Performing any service** (literally, *doing anything*) **secretly without the bishop** points to a divisive presbyter (see comments on 6.1—8.2). The Greek word used here for **worshiping** includes *serving liturgically* (cf. Phil 2.1).

PRAISING THE CHURCH AT SMYRNA

2. May all things, then, abound in grace for you, for you are worthy. In every way you refreshed me; in turn, may Jesus Christ refresh you. In my absence and in my presence you loved me. Your reward is God; if for his sake you patiently endure all things, you shall get to him.

10

1. You did well to welcome Philo and Rheus Agathopus, who followed me for God's sake, as deacons of God. They too give thanks to the Lord on your behalf because you refreshed them in every way. Surely none of this shall be lost to you.

2. My spirit is an offering devoted to you, and so are my chains. You did not despise them, nor were you ashamed of them, so the perfect hope, Jesus Christ, shall not be ashamed of you.

SENDING AN ENVOY TO THE CHURCH AT ANTIOCH

11

1. Your prayer has gone forth to the church at Antioch in Syria. Having come from there as a criminal bound in chains most pleasing to God, I embrace everyone, even though I am not worthy to be from there, since I am the least of them. Yet by his will I was counted worthy, not because of conscientiousness, but by the grace of God. My request is that this grace may be given to me in perfect measure, so that by your prayer I may attain to God.

PRAISING THE CHURCH AT SMYRNA

2. A Christian's **abundance** is **in grace** (cf. Sal, 6.2). Hospitable **love** that **refreshes** others is part of this. **If we move in grace**, we move toward **God**. And **if** it is **for his sake** that we **endure all things, we shall** gain **him** as our **reward** (Mag 1.2; for more on **getting to God**, see Eph 10.1).

10

1. The same word is used for **give thanks** and *celebrate the Eucharist,* so Ignatius may have in mind **Deacons Philo and Rheus Agathopus** (mentioned in Phld 11.1) assisting in the *celebration of the Eucharist* **on behalf** of others. As for the **refreshing** hospitality of the Smyrnaeans, their "reward" (9.2) for **this shall not** *perish.*

2. Ignatius **is devoted to** them to the point of **offering** his own life in death (Eph 21.1; Pol 2.3, 6.1; Eph 7.2). The Smyrnaeans are **not ashamed of** the convict's **chains, so Jesus Christ shall not be ashamed of** them. He is **the perfect hope** of those who **offer** their lives sacrificially in **spirit** and in flesh.

SENDING AN ENVOY TO THE CHURCH AT ANTIOCH

11

1. **Chains most pleasing to God** remind us of Christ and his saints **pleasing God** by limiting themselves for our sakes. In keeping with Paul's words that "**by grace** you have been saved through faith, and that not of yourselves, it is the **gift** of God" (Eph 2:8, Phil 1.3), Ignatius affirms that **God's grace** is the basis of our **worthiness** and the means for our **attaining to God. Conscientiousness** (or *conscience*) matters, but it is nothing without **the grace of God**, without which our sacrifice cannot be **perfected** (11.2–3, Phld 5.1, Rom 1.2).

2. So, then, in order that your work may reach its perfect completion both on earth and in heaven, it is right that your church appoint for the honor of God a godly envoy to travel to Syria and congratulate them on being at peace, on having recovered their proper greatness, and on having had restored to them their proper corporate condition.

3. So it appeared to me a deed worthy of God to send one of your own with an epistle. That way he might join in extolling the divine calm that has come to them and exult with them in their having now reached a safe harbor by your prayer. Inasmuch as you are mature, think about bringing your plans to maturity also. For if you want to do right, God stands ready to help.

FINAL EXHORTATIONS, REQUEST FOR PRAYER, AND FAREWELL

12

1. The love of the brothers and sisters in Troas embraces you. From there also I am writing you through Burrhus. Together with the Ephesians, your brothers and sisters, you sent him along with me, and he has in every way refreshed me. O that everyone would imitate him, since he is a model example of service to God. Grace will reward him in every circumstance.

2. Christian **perfection** requires fraternal love between **churches**. The **church** at Antioch has overcome its conflict and is now **at peace** (Phld 10.1, Pol 7.1–2). **Greatness** is a quality **proper** to an exemplary **church** (Eph Sal), one "not only called Christian," but one that has "proved to be" such (Rom 3.2). **Corporate condition** is about the **church's** unity as a *body* and how healthy it is. **Restored condition** means the return to a vigorous constitution. Problems from persecution have been healed, as well as any connected with Jewish-Gentile relations and the possible choice of the next bishop (Phld 10.1, Sm 1.2, Pol 7.1–2, Rom 9.1).

3. **An epistle** is a formal letter with personal salutations and instruction. Ignatius now describes the "peace" he mentioned above (11.2) as **the divine calm** after the storm of conflict and as the **safe harbor** of unity that **they have reached** (cf. Pol 2.3). Out of their **mature** (or *perfect*) character they are to **bring to maturity** (or *perfection*) their **plans** to send "a godly envoy" (11.2). The word for **help** contains the idea that "**God** will *supply*" whatever we "*need*" **to do** what is **right** (Phil 4:19).

FINAL EXHORTATIONS, REQUEST
FOR PRAYER, AND FAREWELL

12

1. Deacon **Burrhus is a model example of service to God** (cf. Eph 2.1, Tr 3.2, Phld 11.2). Consequently, **everyone**—those who have remained, those who have left, and those who have reconciled—should **imitate him**. To live the Christian life is to **serve**. Insofar as each of us is **a model servant**, we too may expect **grace** to **reward** us **in every circumstance** (or *in every way*). To **serve** others as **Burrhus's** Master did—who "came to serve, rather than be served"—will cost us our lives, but may "ransom many" from destruction (Matt 20:28).

2. I embrace your God-worthy bishop and God-pleasing council of presbyters, as well as my fellow slaves, the deacons, and all of you individually and collectively, in the name of Jesus Christ and in his flesh and blood, by both his passion and his physical and spiritual resurrection, in unity with God and with you. May grace, mercy, peace, and patient endurance be yours continuously.

13

1. I embrace the households of my brothers, together with their wives and children, as well as the virgins who are called widows. May you fare well, I say, in the Father's power. Philo, who is with me, embraces you.

2. I embrace the household of Gavia. My request is for her to be firmly established in faith and love, both physically and spiritually. I embrace Alce, whose name is very dear to me, along with the incomparable Daphnus, as well as Eutecnus and everyone else. May you fare well in the grace of God.

2. St. Polycarp is their **God-worthy bishop**. **God's** own **unity** is central to their church's **unity** and everything else that Ignatius mentions here: their **godly** leadership, their **individual and collective** identity as Christians, the **flesh and blood of Jesus Christ**, and **his passion and resurrection**. Within this **unity, grace, mercy, peace,** and **patience** are ours **continuously**—yea *forever*! We need to **unite** ourselves to these *divine* energies in our own **physical** (*fleshy*) and **spiritual** *suffering* (**passion**), so that we may reach our own **physical and spiritual resurrection** (John 5:21–29, 1 Cor 15:35–44, Ag Heresies 5.7) and arrive at that "*unity* which is **God** himself" (Tr 11.1–2, Phld 9.1). When Ignatius calls **deacons** his **fellow slaves**, he may be fondly remembering his service as a **deacon**, which was and is the first major step to becoming a bishop (see Eph 2.1, Mag 2.1, Phld 4.1, Tr 3.1–2).

13

1. By **virgins**, Ignatius means women who have consecrated themselves to Christ (Pol 5.2). Having outlived their relatives, they now are treated as **widows** with no **household** to care for them (on the Church's care for **widows**, see 1 Tim 5:3–16, especially verses 8 and 16 about the care of **widows** within **households**). **Philo** is the deacon mentioned earlier (10.1, Phld 11.1).

2. Christian **faith and love** are not merely **spiritual**. They must be expressed **physically**, through our *flesh*. Otherwise, all of us, including **Gavia** will only seem **spiritual**, like the Docetists. As for Ignatius's closing sentence, it is only **in the grace of God** that we can ever **fare well**.

The Epistle of St. Ignatius to St. Polycarp

CONTENTS

SALUTATION

Ignatius the God-bearer to Polycarp, bishop of the church of the Smyrnae-ans—or rather, to him who is overseen by God the Father and the Lord Jesus Christ. Abundant greetings.

EXHORTATION TO BISHOP POLYCARP

1

1. I welcome your godly mindset that is firmly settled as if upon an immovable rock. And I offer boundless and glorious praise that I was counted worthy of seeing your blameless face. May I draw joy from it in God.

2. I encourage you, by the grace with which you are clothed, to press forward in your race and to encourage all people to be saved. Do justice to your position with constant care for both physical and spiritual concerns. Be mindful of union, for there is nothing better. Bear with everybody, even as the Lord bears with you. Put up with everyone in love, just as you already do.

SALUTATION

Is overseen by can also be rendered *has as bishop* or *is watched over by*. **God the Father and the Lord Jesus Christ** are so united as to have a single *oversight* (cf. Rom 9.1, 1 Pet 2:25, Pol 8.3, Mag 3.1).

EXHORTATION TO BISHOP POLYCARP

1

1. Polycarp has the **mindset** of the man whose house was **firmly settled**—in fact, *founded*—**"upon a rock"** (Matt 7:24–25; regarding Polycarp's episcopal office, see Matt 16:18). As Ignatius puts it at the end of this epistle, Polycarp is a man who has acquired "God's **mindset**" (8.1, 1.3; Mag 15.1; Rom 3.2). Like **a rock**, he is **immovable**, imperturbable (Mart Pol 13.3, 1 Cor 15:58). His is the **joyful, blameless face** of a **godly** saint (on Moses's "**glorified** face," see Exod 34:29–35), which is itself an **offering** of **glorious praise** to our **God** (Tr 1.2).

2. An alternate translation for **encourage** is *exhort*. **Are clothed** (passive voice) can also be understood as *have clothed yourself* (middle voice). **Race** refers to the Christian life (Eph 3.1—4.1, Phld 2.2). **Physical** (literally, *fleshy*) includes the *material*. To **care for** his people, Polycarp must **be mindful of** (and *focus* his *attention on*) their **union** (or *unity*). Ignatius says of this **union**, of the "peace" Christ brings (Eph 13.2), and of "Christ" himself (Mag 7.1), that **there is nothing better**. He can say this of **union** and peace because they embody who Christ is (Eph 2:14–16, Isa 9:6–7/9:5–6 OSB). Protecting and promoting this God-given *unity* requires each of us to **bear with everybody** and **put up with** them. Polycarp was **doing** this **with** his flock, ever **mindful** that **the Lord** was **already doing** this **with** him.

3. Spend the time at your disposal on unceasing prayers. Ask for understanding greater than you have. Keep awake the unsleeping spirit you possess by acquisition. Speak to the people individually in accordance with the godly convictions and habits that you share in common. Bear the illnesses of all as a perfect athlete. Where there is more strain, there is great gain.

2

1. If you should happen to show affection to good disciples, it is no credit to you. Instead, with meekness bring those who are more troublesome to a place of freely-chosen cooperation. Not every wound is healed by the same plaster. Relieve fits of irritation with soothing applications.

2. Among all sorts of people "become as shrewd as the serpent, yet" ever "harmless as the dove." The reason you are physical, as well as spiritual, is so that you may gently handle what is visibly apparent to you. But pray for what is invisible to become apparent to you, so that you may lack nothing and abound in every spiritual gift.

3. **Spend the time at your disposal on** can also be translated *Devote your-selves to.* This may (as in 1 Cor 7:5) include fasting. (Regarding **spending time** on **unceasing prayers**, see 1 Thess 5:17; Luke 18:1; Eph 10.1, 15.2; Phil 4.3, 8.1; on **spending time** in service to God, see Pol 7.3, Tr 2.2, Eph 9.1.) By his ascetical **straining** as **an athlete** of Christ, Polycarp **has** managed to **acquire** what the disciples did not have in the Garden of Gethsemane: an **unsleeping spirit** (Matt 26:36–43, Eph 1.1, Mag 15.1, Mart Pol 18.3). As a result, **great gain** has come to the **athlete** Polycarp and his flock, who have been relieved of their **illnesses** of soul and body by his **bearing** them (2.1–2, 1.2; Matt 8:17; Gal 6:2). What Polycarp has **acquired** by **straining** is still a gift of grace, whether we say that God has "clothed" him "with grace"—God's magnificent part, or the saint has "clothed" himself "with grace"—his significant part (1.2).

2

1. Ignatius had just spoken of Polycarp "bearing the illnesses of" his flock (1.3). Now he applies medical terminology to the curing of souls. Every church has some **more troublesome** and **irritable** members who need more time from their pastor than others. **No credit** is due for helping **good disciples** (cf. Luke 6:32). The root for **troublesome** means *plague* or *pestilence.* **Freely-chosen cooperation** is synonymous with *"voluntary sub-mission,"* an alternate translation for "voluntary obedience" (Eph 2.2, Phil 10.2). A **plaster** is a dressing that either hardens to protect or has medicine to heal. Literally, **fits of irritation** are *paroxysms.* **Soothing applications** (*embrocations*) use liniment or lotion. In the sacrament of confession, the Orthodox Church offers her members healing for their souls.

2. In the counsel to be **shrewd** and **harmless**, the influence of the Evange-list Matthew continues (Matt 10:16). The **physical** (*fleshy*) body can **gently handle what is visibly** in need of healing. The **spiritual** eye by **spiritual gift** can see **what is invisible become apparent** in the case of **all sorts of people** and *in all circumstances.* This could involve "a word of wisdom," "a word of knowledge," "gifts of healing" or "occasions requiring discerning of spirits" (1 Cor 12:8–10). Through **prayer**, Polycarp will **lack nothing** for curing the souls of his flock (see 2.1). By his **abounding in every spiritual gift** (*charism*; for more on *charism*, see Eph 1.3, 2.02; Phld Sal; Mart Pol 16.2), his people may "**abound**" more "**in grace**" (Sm 9.2, 2 Cor 9:8, Rom 5:20).

3. Just as pilots rely on winds and the storm-tossed sailor requires a harbor, so the current moment depends on you utterly attaining to God. Be alert as God's athlete. The prize is incorruptibility and eternal life, about which you are already convinced. As for me, my life is an offering devoted to you in every way, and so are my chains, which you have loved.

3

1. Do not let those who seem trustworthy, and yet are promoting strange teachings, strike you with confusion. Stand firm like an anvil being hammered. It is the mark of a great athlete to be bruised and yet triumph. But especially for God's sake, we must patiently endure all things, so that he may patiently endure us as well.

2. Become more eager in exerting effort than you are. Carefully notice opportunities.

Expectantly wait for him who is
above the moment,
beyond time,
invisible,
who for our sakes became visible,
beyond touch,
above suffering,
who for our sakes was subject to suffering,
who in every way for our sakes endured.

3. **Utterly attaining to God** starts now. Every **moment** (or *occasion*) is an *opportunity* for St. Polycarp—and each and every one of us—to reach out and *reach* **God** in the midst of this life's adversities (cf. 3.1, Sm 4.2). His flock is **depending on** him—and others are on us. They need an able pastor for them to avoid being "tossed to and fro by waves and carried about with every **wind** of teaching by the trickery of men" (Eph 4:14). For him to effectively **pilot** his church and provide safe **harbor** to **the storm-tossed** who live in his port city, he must **be alert as God's athlete** (cf. 1.3, 3.1, 6.1; Sm 11.3; Mart Pol 2.1, 18.3; 1 Clem 5.1). To **be alert** is to *be sober-minded* and *clear-headed* (for more on this, see Sm 9.1, Phil 11.3). For St. Ignatius, being **devoted in every way** includes **offering** his **life** in the arena so that the Romans might not come after his flock (Eph 21.1). Later on, Polycarp himself will be the one to *give his life* for others (Mart Pol 1.1). By his martyrdom, he will **utterly attain to God** and win **the prize** of "**incorruptibility**" and "**eternal life**" (Mart Pol 14.2).

3

1. **Those who seem** are the Docetists. **Strange teachings** are the same as "heterodox teachings" (Mag 8.1), "heterodox approaches" (Sm 6.2), and "heresy" found in "**strange**" communities (Tr 6.1). **God's athlete** will be attacked by the devil with **confusion**, and **be hammered** and **bruised**, but as he **endures all things**, God himself will **patiently** support him **and** he will "**triumph**" (4 Macc 6:10, 17:15). **Athletes** in this world "strain" for one reason: to "win" their contests, **but** the goal for Christians is pleasing **God**, not achieving success or impressing people (cf. 1.3, 2.3; Phld 2.2).

2. Here may be another hymn of Christ (cf. Eph 7.2). Greek has two words for time. *Kairos* is a "**moment**" (2.3) that can be described, such as a special *occasion* in one's life. Christ is **above** such time and always here to help. **Opportunities** refer to those **moments** where we need to **more eagerly exert effort**. *Chronos* is **time** that can be counted. Christ is **beyond** *chronological* **time**, and so is always on **time**. But he became **visible** and **subject to suffering** for our sakes in our **time**-bound world. Now untouchable by his enemies, our enthroned Lord can help us make the best of every **opportunity** when we **wait for him** expectantly.

4

1. Do not let the widows be neglected. After the Lord, you yourself must be their guardian. Nothing is to be done without your consent, and you yourself must not do anything without God's consent, which is not your practice anyway. Keep standing firm.

2. Hold meetings that are closer together. Seek out everyone by name.

3. Do not treat male or female slaves with contempt, but neither let them be puffed up. Rather, let them serve devotedly for the glory of God, that they may obtain from God a better freedom. Do not let them burn to be set free out of the common fund, lest they be found to be slaves of lust.

5

1. Shun the base occupations; do even more and preach a sermon about them. Tell my sisters to love the Lord and be satisfied with their husbands in flesh and spirit. Likewise instruct my brothers in the name of Jesus Christ to "love" their "wives as" the Lord "loved the Church."

4

1. A **guardian** is *a person responsible for the welfare of others.* Leaders must be careful in giving their **consent** (cf. 5.2). **Standing firm** in a port city requires *being even-keeled, steady,* and *calm* (cf. 2.3, Sm 11.3).

2. Being **closer** can involve *more frequent* and *tighter-knit* **meetings** (Eph 13.1, Heb 10:25). Orthodox clergy show their **closeness** with **everyone** by serving the Eucharist to each of them "**by name**" (Eph 20.2).

3. **Slaves** must not **serve** for their owner's **contemptible** vain**glory** or their own **puffed-up glory**, but *instead* **for God's glory.** The church's treasury, its **common fund**, is for needs, not individual wants that **burn** to be obliged. Ignatius may have feared **freed slaves** would turn to the "base occupation" of prostitution (5.1) for survival in a world with little place for them (for more on **slaves** in Smyrna, see Mart Pol 6.1—7.1).

5

1. Prostitution is one of **the base occupations** Polycarp is to **shun and preach about**. Married **sisters** should **love the Lord and be satisfied with their husbands in flesh** (*sexually* and *materially*) **and spirit** (*spiritually*). **Likewise** married **brothers** are **to "love" their "wives as** Christ **loved the Church** and gave himself for her" sacrificially unto death (Eph 5:25).

2. If anyone is able to continue in sexual purity in honor of the Lord's flesh, let him do so without boasting. But if he should ever boast, he is lost. And should it become known beyond the bishop, he is ruined. Now it is right for men and women who are marrying to be united with the bishop's consent, that the marriage may be in line with the Lord, and not in line with lust. Let everything be done in honor of God.

EXHORTATION TO THE SMYRNAEANS

6

1. You all must give heed to the bishop, so that God may also give heed to you. As for me, my life is devoted to those who freely submit themselves to the bishop, presbyters, and deacons. May it be granted me to have my place with them near God. Keep training hard together with each other, contending together as athletes, running together, suffering together, sleeping together, and rising up together as God's stewards, attendants, and assistants.

2. Whatever we do **sexually** should **honor God**. Here **sexual purity** refers to a life consecrated to *chastity* (Sm 13.1). **Marrying** is better than **purity boasted** and **lost** (cf. 1 Clem 38.2). Let us not forget that "pride goeth before a fall" (Prov 16:18/16:16 OSB). **The bishop's consent** is important for the couple getting **married**. Likewise **the bishop** is important as confidant and confessor to the one who **boasts**, so that **it** (either **loss** of **purity** or **boast** of *chastity*) might not be **known beyond the bishop** (cf. Phld 8.1). **Ruined** is elsewhere translated *corrupted*. Our **marriages** must please **the Lord** and avoid anything that is **in line with lust** (Tob 8:7, 1 Thess 4:3–7, Heb 13:4). Ignatius concludes his exhortations to various groups (4.1—5.2) with these words: **Let everything be done in honor of God.** This stands in stark contrast to the Roman preoccupation with one's own **honor**. Unmindful of himself, Ignatius had **boasted** of being "counted worthy to be found serving **God's honor** in chains" (Eph 21.2). He speaks of the Father's **honor** and our **Lord's honor** (Eph 21.1–2; Mag 3.2, 15; Tr 12.2; Sm 11.2). We **honor God** and **the Lord**—and they **honor** us—when we serve them and support our leaders (Eph 2.1, 21.1–2; Mag 3.2; Tr 12.2; Phld 11.2; Sm 9.1, 11.2; Mart Pol 13.2).

EXHORTATION TO THE SMYRNAEANS

6

1. From this point on, Ignatius directly addresses the Smyrnaeans as a group, using **you all** instead of *you*. He first exhorts them to **give heed to Bishop** Polycarp. If they do, it will be because they **freely submit themselves to** him and his **presbyters and deacons** (cf. Phil 5.3). Ignatius seems more confident that those who **give heed** will **have** their **place near God** than that he will (on his **devotion to them**, see Eph 21.1, Sm 10.2, Pol 2.3). He especially encourages **them** to **train hard together** as **athletes**, so they may be prepared by practice to **suffer** (unto death if need be), **sleep** (rest or die), and **rise up together** (now and at the resurrection) to serve **as God's** ministers, whether on earth or in heaven (cf. Mag 11.1 on our experiencing the passion and resurrection). St. Ignatius had likewise urged St. Polycarp to be "God's **athlete**" (2.3). This **lifelong training** is done **together** and will make **them** all battle-**hardened** "soldiers" (6.2) for this **life** and the next.

2. Keep on pleasing him whom you serve as soldiers. Let none of you be found to be a deserter. Let your baptism remain as an arsenal of weapons, while you keep using faith for a helmet, love for a spear, and endurance for a full set of armor. Let your deeds be your deposits, that you may draw the credited back pay you deserve. Therefore, be long-suffering with one another in a meek manner, since God is with you. May I always draw joy from you.

SENDING ENVOYS TO THE CHURCH AT ANTIOCH

7

1. Since, as reported to me, the church at Antioch in Syria is at peace because of your prayer, I too am in better spirits in a God-given freedom from care, provided, of course, that through the suffering of martyrdom I attain to God—and thus prove to be a disciple by your entreaty.

2. It is appropriate, O Polycarp most blessed of God, to convene a most God-pleasing council and to appoint someone whom you all hold to be especially loved and not given to shrinking back, someone who is qualified to be called God's courier. Count that one worthy of going to Syria, that he may glorify your community's love that does not shrink back, and thus bring glory to God.

3. A Christian exercises no authority over himself, but instead spends the time at his disposal for God. This deed belongs to God, as well as to all of you, whenever you complete it. For I am relying on grace that you are ready to do what is right when it involves God. Knowing your fervor for the truth, I have exhorted you all in just a few lines.

2. In **baptism** we are enlisted as **soldiers** (cf. 2 Tim 2:3–5). We must **remain in God's service** or we will become **deserters**. Our **baptism** supplies us with all the *military hardware* we need for offense and defense, so that "together" (6.1) we may **serve him**. For **a spear** we can use **love** with which to penetrate the hearts of our foes. When a Roman soldier was given bonuses, half was given at the time; the other half was put on **deposit** and **credited** as **back pay** to be **drawn** if he completed his **service** honorably. The Smyrnaeans can expect their full **back pay** if their **deeds** of **faith** show they are still **with God** (cf. Eph 8.2).

SENDING ENVOYS TO THE CHURCH AT ANTIOCH

7

1. Our **prayer** for others can put our clergy **in better spirits** (on **at peace**, see Phld 10.1, Sm 11.2, Tr Sal). **Your** is plural throughout this chapter. The conditional clause **provided, of course. . .I attain** can also be translated *in the hope that. . .I may attain*. Literally, **the suffering of martyrdom** is either **the suffering** [by Ignatius] or the *passion* [of Christ] (Tr 4.2, Rom 6.3). Either way, Ignatius intends to unite his **suffering** in **martyrdom** to **the suffering** of Christ in order that he may **attain to God** (Phil 3:10, Col 1:24, 2 Cor 1:5). May we too **prove to be disciples**, not "deserters" (6.2).

2. This communication is in keeping with Greek inter-city diplomacy (cf. Sm 11.2–3, Phld 10.1–2). Bishop **Polycarp** and his **council** of presbyters (Phil Sal; Sm 8.1; Phld Sal, 8.1–2) will send a **courier** whom their **community** endorses. His sending will be a united effort in support of unity within the church at Antioch and between her and her sister churches. The **courier** has the **qualification of not being one to shrink back**. This may be because his **love**, like theirs, is **not** one **to shrink back**.

3. We must put all our **time at God's disposal** (1.3; for more on our use of **time**, see Pol 3.2). The courier and Smyrnaeans will **do** this to **complete** their good **deed** of sending an embassy to Antioch. **Relying on grace** is essential to **doing what is right**. **Fervor for the truth** may refer to their *zeal* for Ignatius's perspective on the earlier problems at "Antioch" that have been resolved in favor of "peace" (7.1–2, Sm 11.1–3).

8

1. I could not write to all the churches because of my sailing at any moment from Troas to Neapolis, as the divine will is directing. Therefore, since you are worthy, will you, as one possessing God's mindset, write to the churches that lie ahead, so that they too may do the same? Those that can should send messengers, while the rest should send epistles through the messengers being sent by you. That way all of you may be glorified by an eternal deed.

FINAL GREETINGS AND FAREWELL

2. I embrace every one of you personally, especially the widow of Epitropus, together with all her household, including the children. I embrace my beloved Attalus. I also embrace the one about to be counted worthy of going to Syria. Grace shall be with him at all times, and with Polycarp, who sends him.

3. I wish that you all may always fare well in our God Jesus Christ. May you all remain in him in the unity and oversight of God. I embrace Alce, whose name is very dear to me. May you all fare well in the Lord.

8

1. Ignatius is about to pass out of Asia (**Troas**) into Europe (**Neapolis**). **Neapolis** was the harbor of Philippi, the city to which St. Paul and St. Polycarp wrote their **epistles**. **You** refers to Polycarp; **all of you** to the Smyrnaeans. **Possessing** can also be translated *who has acquired*. Ignatius had only **written** his request for envoys to Smyrna (11.1–3) and to Philadelphia (10.1–2). Now he humbly asks the **worthy** Polycarp to finish contacting all **the** remaining **churches that lie ahead** of Smyrna on the way to Antioch, namely, those at Ephesus, Magnesia, and Tralles. **Doing the same** and the **eternal deed** are the **sending** of **messengers** and **epistles** to the church at Antioch (7.1–3, Phil 13.1).

FINAL GREETINGS AND FAREWELL

2. Literally, **personally** is *by name* (see Eph 20.2, Pol 4.2, 3 John 14). **Epitropus** can be a name, and most translators take it that way. Usually it is a title for a Roman administrator and is then translated *procurator*. This **widow** might be the wealthy patron of their **house** church and could even be the Gavia that Ignatius mentioned previously (Sm 13.2).

3. This **oversight** comes from **God** who **oversees** and their bishop through whom **God oversees**. Their **unity** includes the **unity** between **our God Jesus Christ** and "**God** the Father" (Pol Sal). It also includes the Holy Spirit within the Triune **God** (Mag 13.1–2). This **unity** is present in their church through **God's** bishop and the ones who are **united** with **God** and him (Phld 7.2—8.1). **Alce** was from Smyrna (13.2, Mart Pol 17.2).

St. Polycarp of Smyrna

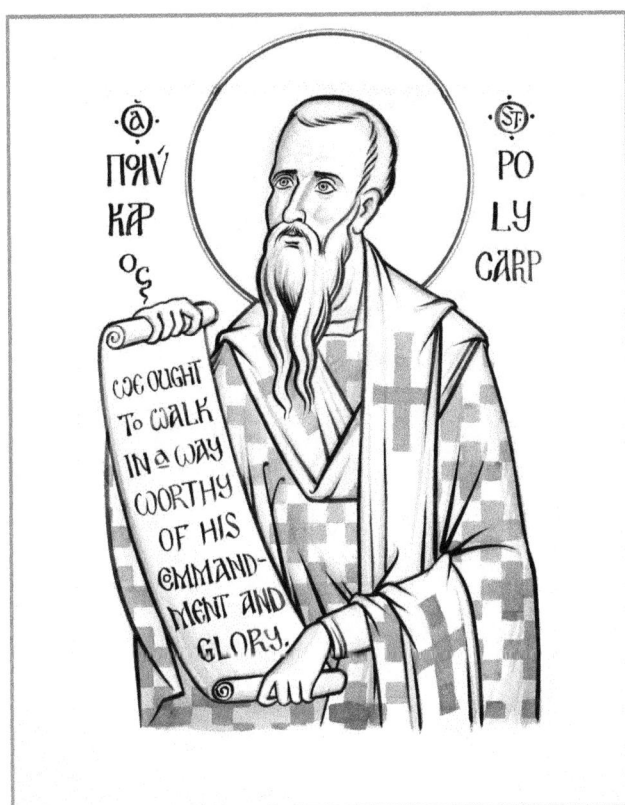

Introduction to St. Polycarp

THE NAME POLYCARP MEANS *much fruit* and well describes the man. He towers over the second-century Church as "an outstanding teacher" and "an eminent martyr" (Mart Pol 19.1). By ascetical labor he came to "possess God's mindset" and became "settled" and "immovable" like a rock (Pol 8.1, 1.1; cf. Sm 1.1). He is the vital link connecting St. John and St. Ignatius, from the first century, to his own disciple, St. Irenaeus, who defended the Church against the Gnostics in the last decades of the second century. St. Polycarp's influence will extend from Smyrna into all Roman Asia,[1] to Philippi in Greece, to Rome in Italy, and, through St. Irenaeus, to Lugdunum in Gaul (Lyons, France).

St. Irenaeus calls his mentor "that blessed and apostolic elder."[2] He recounts how Polycarp had interacted with John and others who were "eyewitnesses of the Word of Life" and had received from them what he taught.[3] *The Prologue from Ochrid* records that John "brought" Polycarp "to the Christian faith and baptized him."[4] The Orthodox *Synaxarion* tells us that Polycarp and Ignatius, were "initiated into the deepest mysteries of the faith by St. John."[5] Polycarp then "made great efforts to emulate the Holy

1. Eusebius calls him "the teacher of Asia" in his excerpts from *The Martyrdom of Polycarp* (Ch Hist 4.15.26, Mart Pol 12.2). "All the churches throughout Asia" bore witness to his fidelity to "what he had learned from the apostles" (Ch Hist 4.14.4–5, Phil 6.3). "He was appointed bishop at the church in Smyrna with a view to Asia" (Ag Heresies 3.3.4; quoted in Ch Hist 4.14.3) and was "principal leader of all Asia" (Lives 17).

2. *Epistle to Florinus* (as found in Ch Hist 5.20.7). Irenaeus may have called Polycarp "that blessed and apostolic elder [presbyter]" because he was an elder in wisdom and elderly in age (see Polycarp Intro, fn. 14; Mag 3.1; Ag Heresies 4.26.2–5).

3. Ch Hist 5.20.6; 1 John 1:1.

4. *The Prologue from Ochrid*: The Hieromartyr Polycarp, Bishop of Smyrna. February 23rd.

5. *The Synaxarion of Holy Hieromartyr Ignatius the God-Bearer of Antioch. December 20.*

Apostles John and Paul, whom he had met and heard."[6] Before Polycarp's bishop died, he named him his successor. Subsequently, he was ordained with apostolic approval.[7]

Many scholars question St. John's influence.[8] Doubting St. Irenaeus's testimony about the relationship between John and Polycarp, they end up differentiating between John the Apostle and John the Elder.[9] But they do recognize the influence of St. Paul's epistles, *First Peter*, and *First Clement* on Polycarp's *Epistle to the Philippians*.[10]

The date of Polycarp's birth is uncertain. If his age was eighty-six at his martyrdom, taking his being saved by Christ to refer to his baptism as an infant (Mart Pol 9.3), and if the most likely date for his martyrdom was 155,[11] then he was born in 69. But this does not allow for his having heard St. Paul, who was martyred under Nero, who died in 68.[12] The *Prologue* says a wealthy lady took him in as an orphaned child, which, if so, would argue against his having been baptized as an infant.[13] Perhaps 69 actually was the date of his baptism, but as a youth, and he was born between 50 and 55.[14]

---

6. *The Prologue from Ochrid*: Polycarp. According to Berding, Polycarp imitated Paul's style in *Philippians* (*Polycarp and Paul*, 127–41).

7. The *Prologue* recounts that Polycarp was "consecrated bishop" by "apostolic bishops" at "the funeral of St. Bucolus," his mentor. Tertullian says John "placed" Polycarp in the church of Smyrna (Prescript 32.2). Irenaeus says he "was appointed bishop by apostles" (Ag Heresies 3.3.4; quoted in Ch Hist 4.14.3). Apostles may have selected him and bishops finally "consecrated" him.

8. On these academic opinions, see Hartog, *Polycarp's Epistle and Martyrdom*, 11–16.

9. Hill, however, credibly argues in favor of Irenaeus's trustworthiness (see Hartog, 12–13 and Hill, *Lost Teaching of Polycarp*, 171–77; also see Polycarp Intro, 158–159, fnn. 14 and 16).

10. See Berding, especially 1–2, 127–41, and 191–205; also see Hartog, 60–68, for an overview of scholarly opinion. After a similar overview for the *Martyrdom of Polycarp* (209–13), Hartog concludes that clear dependence on specific New Testament writings is lacking in that text, but the use of many allusions points to the kind of literary influence typical of hagiographical literature (212). A number of these allusions, as the commentary below will show, are Johannine. Also see Polycarp Intro, 159, fn. 23.

11. See text and comments on Mart Pol 21.1; also see Polycarp Intro, 160, fn. 26.

12. *The Prologue from Ochrid*: Polycarp; also see Ignatius Intro, 3, fn. 1, and Polycarp Intro, 158, fn. 6.

13. *The Prologue from Ochrid*: Polycarp; also see Polycarp Intro, 157, fn. 4. According to Pionius, a wealthy Christian lady bought him as a young slave (Life Pol 3).

14. A birth in the early 50s would have allowed Polycarp to hear Paul during his missionary journeys and made him young enough to learn from eyewitnesses to the Lord what he later taught as bishop (see fn. 3). The *Martyrdom* says he was "an elderly man"

This would fit well with the long-standing esteem that one senses between St. Ignatius and St. Polycarp[15] (Mag 15.1; Pol Sal, 1.1–3, 2.3, 7.2, 8.2; Phil 9.1, 13.1–2). Then, indeed, would he have been "a right godly old man" at the time of his arrest (Mart Pol 7.3).

His *Epistle to the Philippians* was written right after Ignatius's epistles in the early second century (Phil 13.2, 9.1–2; Rom 10.2). Irenaeus says that Polycarp also wrote other epistles to churches and individuals[16], but we no longer have them. It has even been argued that Polycarp may have been the author of *The Epistle to Diognetus*.[17]

Oral teaching from St. Polycarp is likely embedded in passages in *Against Heresies* 4.27–32 where St. Irenaeus cites an apostolic elder.[18] He used to listen to Polycarp when he was growing up in Smyrna, probably in his late teens and early twenties.[19] He had committed to memory what he said and was still "ruminating" on his words in the late second century.[20]

Polycarp was an implacable foe of Valentinus and Marcion.[21] When asked in Rome by the latter to recognize him, he replied, "I do recognize you. I recognize the firstborn of Satan!"[22] In his earlier words to the Philippians—"Whoever twists the sayings of the Lord to suit his own sordid desires is a firstborn of Satan" (7.1)—we see a prescient mindset that would later oppose Marcion's snippety canon of limited New Testament writings. Polycarp himself "was deeply involved in. . .the formation of the [New Testament] canon."[23] During his visit to Rome around 154 or 155, "he turned

---

(7.2). Irenaeus says Polycarp had "lived for a long time, and was in extreme old age" when he was martyred (Ag Heresies 3.3.4; quoted in Ch Hist 4.14.4). Even in ancient times the well-off might live to quite an advanced age. For what it's worth, the much-criticized Harris Fragments place Polycarp's age at death as 104 (as cited in Hill, 74, fn. 9).

15. Ignatius never calls Polycarp a "young bishop" (cf. Mag 3.1).

16. *Epistle to Florinus* (as found in Ch Hist 5.20.8).

17. Hill, 95–177. Whether or not Polycarp was the author, Hill at least shows that he was an accomplished rhetorician (168–70).

18. Hill, 1–94; also see Polycarp Intro, 157–158, fnn. 2 and 9.

19. Ch Hist 5.20.7, Hill, 74, Ag Heresies 3.3.4, Mart Pol Mosc 22.2. Hill thinks Irenaeus was probably born around 130–35.

20. *Epistle to Florinus* (as found in Ch Hist 5.20.7).

21. Ag Heresies 3.3.4, Phil 7.1.

22. Ag Heresies 3.3.4, Mart Pol Mosc 22.3, Ch Hist 4.14.7.

23. Holmes, *The Apostolic Fathers*, 272. The scriptures cited in our commentary on *The Epistle to the Philippians* reflect Polycarp's broad knowledge of New Testament books (Phil 12.1).

many to the Church" who had been deluded by heretics.[24] And at that time, Pope Anicetus "yielded the celebration of the Eucharist to Polycarp," despite differences over when to observe Pascha (Easter).[25]

Soon after returning from Rome, Polycarp was martyred at Smyrna. Several dates have been proposed for his death with 155 and 156 having the broadest scholarly support.[26] *The Martyrdom of Polycarp*, which records his arrest, interrogation, and martyrdom, was written soon after his death, maybe within a year.[27] According to Holmes, it is "the oldest written account of a Christian martyrdom outside the New Testament" and "was the model" for later accounts of "martyrdom."[28] The text has come down to us through the labors of St. Irenaeus (Mart Pol 22.2–3, Mosc 22.1–5).

St. Polycarp was a powerful man of prayer. In behalf of the Christians in Philippi he prayed thus:

> Now may the God and Father of our Lord Jesus Christ, and the eternal High Priest himself, the Son of God, Jesus Christ, build you up in faith and truth.... May he grant you a share and a place among his saints, and to us together with you, and to all those under heaven who will come to believe in our Lord and God Jesus Christ and in his Father, who raised him from the dead. (Phil 12.2)

At his arrest, he asked leave to pray from those sent to apprehend him. As he stood in prayer,

> he was so full of the grace of God that for two hours he could not keep silent. . . [He] remembered every single person who had ever [been] with him, both small and great, illustrious and obscure, and the entire Catholic Church. (Mart Pol 7.3—8.1)

When he was bound for execution,

> He looked up to heaven and said, "O Lord God Almighty, Father of your beloved and blessed Son, Jesus Christ, through whom we have received full knowledge of you. . . .I bless you because you have counted me worthy of this day and hour to receive a place

24. Ag Heresies 3.3.4. Regarding the date, see Holmes, 301.

25. Ch Hist 5.24.17. For more on the Quartodeciman Controversy, including St. Irenaeus's part in it, see all of chapters 5.23—5.24.

26. Hartog, 191–200, especially 193–94. In 156, the martyrdom would have been on February 22, not 23 (Mart Pol 21.1, 8.1).

27. Mart Pol 18.3; for scholarly views, see Hartog, 171–86.

28. Holmes, 298.

among the number of the martyrs in the cup of your Christ, and thus to share in the resurrection to eternal life, both of soul and of body, in the incorruptibility of the Holy Spirit. May I be admitted among them in your presence today as a sacrifice that is fat and acceptable...For this reason, and for all things, I praise you, I bless you, I glorify you through the eternal and heavenly High Priest, Jesus Christ, your beloved Son, through whom be glory to you together with him and the Holy Spirit, both now and unto the ages to come. Amen." (Mart Pol 14.1–3)

May we who read Polycarp's words today follow his advice that is at once old and yet timeless:

> Forsaking the vanity of the masses and their false teachings, let us turn toward the message handed down to us from the beginning, taking the prayers seriously and adhering to fast days, entreating with supplications the all-seeing God "to lead us not into temptation." (Phil 7.2)

And by "following in his footsteps," may we arrive in Christ's kingdom. (Mart Pol 22.1).

APOLYTIKION IN THE FOURTH TONE[29]

By sharing in the ways of the apostles, you became a successor to their throne. Through the practice of virtue, you found the way to divine contemplation, O inspired one of God; by teaching the word of truth without error, you defended the faith, even to the shedding of your blood. O Hieromartyr Polycarp, entreat Christ God to save our souls.

KONTAKION IN THE FIRST TONE[30]

Through your virtues, O wise Polycarp, you offer spiritual fruits to the Lord and prove to be God's worthy hierarch. We who have been enlightened by your words today praise your memory and glorify God.

---

29. https://www.oca.org/saints/troparia/2022/02/23/100589-hieromartyr-polycarp-bishop-of-smyrna.

30. http://ww1.antiochian.org/node/25312.

The Epistle of St. Polycarp to the Philippians

CONTENTS

SALUTATION

Polycarp and the presbyters with him to the church of God sojourning at Philippi. May mercy and peace from God Almighty and Jesus Christ our Savior be multiplied to you.

REASONS FOR REJOICING

1

1. I greatly rejoice with you in our Lord Jesus Christ that you welcomed the representations of true love and that you helped on their way, as you had opportunity, those who were confined in chains suitable for saints. These chains are the diadems of those truly chosen by God and our Lord.

2. I also rejoice that the firm root of your faith, well-known from earliest times, remains until now and bears fruit for our Lord Jesus Christ. For our sins he patiently endured to the point of facing Death, and God loosed the birth pangs of Hades and raised him up.

SALUTATION

The church at Philippi was the first church in Europe and the recipient of Paul's *Epistle to the Philippians*. Strangers that travel in a foreign land are **sojourners** there (Heb 11:8–10, 1 Pet 1:17). Paul told the **Philippians** "our citizenship is in heaven" (Phil 3:20) and that "as citizens" of the heavenly city we are to "conduct our lives" on earth "in a manner worthy of the gospel of Christ" (Phil 1:27; Phil 5.2; Diogn 5.1–5, 9). **Presbyters with him** refers to **presbyters** who serve as a council **with** Bishop **Polycarp** (Pol 7.2). While he does not call himself bishop, others do (Mag 15.1, Pol Sal, Mart Pol Mosc 22.2), and he was in charge of sending the courier to Syria (Pol 8.2). Only in connection with his imminent martyrdom had Ignatius even called himself bishop (Rom 2.2, 9.1). Instead of demanding obedience, Ignatius was a model example of humility, lording his position over no one (Eph 2.1—3.2, 1 Pet 5:2–5, Matt 20:25). For him—as well as Polycarp—being a bishop meant leading the way in "dying to *reach* Jesus Christ" (Rom 6.1, Mart Pol 1.1–2).

REASONS FOR REJOICING

1

1. **The representations** (or *imitations*) **of true love** are Ignatius and his companions, who passed through Philippi in **chains** (9.1, 8.2). They were **truly chosen** because they made their "*election* sure" by their **love** (2 Pet 1:10). **True love** calls to mind **Love** Incarnate, Jesus Christ (see Rom 7.2 on Ignatius's "passionate desire"). **Chains suitable for saints** are those worn by martyrs for **our Lord's** sake (for "**chains** as spiritual pearls," see Eph 11.2). **Diadems** were a type of crown worn by monarchs in the East. They consisted of a cloth adorned with jewels that was bound about the head, just like **chains** would be bound around the body.

2. **Faith** that **remains firmly rooted** will continue to **bear fruit** (cf. Col 2:6–7). **Our Lord patiently endured** the cross and stared **Death** in the face. Because of him, **Hades** was in distressing **birth pangs** until it was delivered of Christ and its captives when **God raised him up** (Acts 2:24, Matt 27:52–53, Mag 9.2; also see Rom 6.1 and Tr 11.2, respectively, regarding the **birth pangs** of St. Ignatius and of **Jesus Christ**).

3. Though you have not seen him, you trust him "with an inexpressible joy that is full of glory." Many long to enter into this joy because they know that "by grace you have been saved, not because of works," but rather by the will of God through Jesus Christ.

RIGHTEOUSNESS IN ACTION

2

1. Therefore, as people prepared for action, serve God in fear and truth. Forsaking the empty, vain talk and error of the masses, "put your faith in him who raised" our Lord Jesus Christ "from the dead and gave him glory" and a throne "at" his "right hand." To him all things in heaven and on earth are subject, and to him every breath offers worship. He is coming as judge of the living and the dead, and his blood God will require of those who disobey him.

2. Now "he who raised" him from the dead "will raise us also," if we would keep doing his will, walking in his commandments, and loving what he loved, while continuing to refrain from all unrighteousness, greediness, love of money, malicious talk, and false witness, and "not returning evil for evil, insult for insult," blow for blow, or curse for curse,

3. Polycarp's quotes from Peter and Paul remind the Philippians of the "inexpressible joy" of their salvation (1 Pet 1:8) which God has **willed** to give them **"by grace" through Jesus Christ** (Eph 2:5, 8–9; Sm 11.1). They are no longer heathen who must propitiate their capricious gods in order to have some chance at receiving mercy based on their futile **works**. **Trust** can also be translated *believe in*.

RIGHTEOUSNESS IN ACTION

2

1. **As people** *ready* **for action** is, literally, *with your loins girded up* (1 Pet 1:13, Eph 6:14). The **service** commanded is that of a slave **acting** upon his master's every word (6.3, Mart Pol 9.3). Later Polycarp will again tell them to **"forsake the masses"** (7.2; cf. Mart Pol 9.2, 10.2). He quotes Peter from **"put your faith in"** to **"gave him glory"** (1 Pet 1:21). The **throne "at"** his **"right hand"** refers to David's messianic prophecy: "The Lord said to my Lord, 'Sit **at** my **right hand** until I make your enemies a footstool for your feet'" (Ps 109/110:1). **Subjection** is forced *submission*. **Offers worship** involves *serving liturgically* (cf. Sm 9.1). **His blood** redeems us or condemns us by our response. To **disobey him** is to disbelieve and disregard **him**.

2. Here Polycarp starts with phrases from Paul (2 Cor 4:14) and ends with lines from Peter (1 Pet 3:9). **If** and **would** express the truth that our story is not yet finished: we must persevere to the end. The contingent word **if** connects the five criteria that show our obedience to, belief in, and regard for Christ that will issue in the Father **raising us also**. These five are **doing his will**, **walking in his commandments**, **loving what he loved** on earth, **refraining from all** vice and viciousness, and "keeping in mind what the Lord said" (2.3). These actions do not earn a right to be resurrected, but they reveal that our faith and **love** are genuine and growing. **Greediness** is, literally, *a desire to possess more*. **Insult** can be translated *reviling* or *tonguelashing*. Here Polycarp hints that the Philippians should not **return evil** to Valens **for** his **greedy** theft (cf. 3.1, 11.1–2).

3. while keeping in mind what the Lord said when he taught: "Judge not, lest you be judged; forgive, and it will be forgiven you; show mercy, so that you may be shown mercy; with the measure you use, it will be measured back to you;" and, "blessed are the poor" and "those persecuted for righteousness's sake, for theirs is the kingdom of God."

3

1. Not on my own initiative, brothers, do I write these things to you about righteousness, but because you invited me yourselves.

2. For neither I, nor another like me, can come close to the wisdom of the blessed and glorious Paul. Back at the time when he was in the presence of your people face to face, he taught accurately and authoritatively the word concerning the truth. When absent, he also wrote epistles to you. If you would closely examine them, you will be able to build yourselves up into the faith that was given to you.

3. This faith is "the mother of us all," while hope follows after, and love directed toward God and Christ and toward our neighbor leads the way. For if anybody be in company with these, he has fulfilled the commandment of righteousness, for the one having love is far from all sin.

3. **Keeping in mind** involves not only *remembering*, but also acting on what we *remember*. **What the Lord taught** is found in the *Gospels of Matthew and Luke*. Part of Polycarp's wording matches theirs exactly, but part is a conflation of their words, perhaps due to his own recollection and recounting, with possible influence from *First Clement* and oral tradition (Matt 7:1–2; Luke 6:36–38, 20; Matt 5:3, 7, 10; 1 Clem 13.1–2).

3

1. Polycarp **writes** the Philippians humbly as a pastor who has been **invited** to answer questions **about** how to respond **righteously** to Valens (11.1—12.1). **Righteousness** points back to the Lord's teaching in 2.3 and Polycarp's counsel in 2.2, and is an overarching theme throughout this epistle (3.3, 7.1—9.1).

2. Here Polycarp humbles himself before **the wisdom of the blessed Paul** (cf. 2 Pet 3:15–16). **Blessed** is an early term for departed saints (Phil 9.1, 11.3; Mart Pol 1.1; 19.1; 21.1; 22.1, 3; Mosc 22.1, 3, 5). The mention of multiple **epistles** by **Paul** to the Philippians may be an example of Greek literature's habit of referring to one **epistle** in the plural. The **epistle** Polycarp had in hand was the same one **Paul** wrote (see 11.3 and references from *Philippians* cited in the commentary). But the Philippians had likely received many of **Paul's** other **epistles**, since the churches circulated these between themselves (Col 4:16; 2 Pet 3:15–16; Phil 13.2, 12.1 comments; Mart Pol 20.1). Literally, **closely examine** means *stoop down and peer into*. As we place ourselves below **the word** of **truth**, we can **build** ourselves **up into the faith** (cf. Jude 3, 20).

3. Paul called the Jerusalem above **"the mother of us all"** (Gal 4:26) because we are her children "by **faith**" (Gal 3:22, 26; 4:22—5:1). **Being in company with "faith, hope, and love"** (1 Cor 13:13) connects us to **God and Christ and neighbor** (cf. Matt 22:34–40). **Love** keeps us **far** *away* **from all sin** (cf. Dem 95, Gal 5:13–24).

4

1. But the beginning of all hard conditions is the love of money. Knowing, then, that "we brought nothing into the world" and, moreover, have "nothing to take out," we must equip ourselves with the weapons of righteousness and first teach ourselves to walk in the commandment of the Lord.

2. Afterward, teach your wives also to walk in the faith, love, and purity given to them, showing tender affection to their own husbands in total fidelity, and showing love to everyone else equally in complete chastity. And teach them to instruct their children with the discipline that instills the fear of God.

3. The widows are to be serious about the faith of the Lord, interceding unceasingly for everyone and staying far away from all slander, malicious talk, false witness, love of money, and every kind of evil. They should act this way knowing that they are God's altar and that he examines every offering for blemishes. Indeed, nothing escapes his notice, neither rationalizations, nor plans, nor any secrets of the heart.

4

1. **The love of money** leads to **hard conditions** (or *hardships*; cf. Mart Pol 11.1, where **love of** power and **money** beget the **condition** of a "**hard heart**"). Attachment to material things detaches us from the "**love**" that "is far from all sin" (3.3; cf. Rom 6.2, 7.2); and it produces "all sorts of evil" (1 Tim 6:10). **Knowing** our **nothingness** (cf. 1 Tim 6:7), let us wield the defensive and offensive **weapons of righteousness** against **our** sinful passions. This accords with Paul's instruction to use such **weapons** to "stand against the devil" (Eph 6:10–17; Pol 6.2; 1 Thess 5:8; Isa 59:16–17; 2 Cor 6:7, 10:3–5). **We** men **must first teach ourselves to walk in the Lord's commandment**. If only Valens had done this and exercised self-control over his **love of money**, what *hardships* might have been avoided (11.1–4).

2. Polycarp probably says **your wives** because he was never married. **Faith, love, and purity** were **given to them** in baptism (3.2, Mag 9.1). **Total fidelity** can be translated *all truth* and **chastity** can be rendered *self-control*. **Instruct** and **child** come from the same Greek root. Hence, through **instruction**, which involves *disciplined practice*, we should lead our **children** forward into **the fear of God** (Eph 6:4; 1 Clem 1.3, 21.6).

3. **The widows** should **be serious about** how they live **the faith** (for what Paul says about **widows**, see 1 Tim 5:3–16, Titus 2:3–5). Employing their tongues in **unceasing intercession** helps them keep **far away from all slander** and other sins of the tongue that can lead to the **love of money** and **every kind of evil**. Every sacrifice we **offer**—whether of intercession or sin-avoidance, or some other—is **examined for blemishes**. **Neither** our **rationalizations, nor plans, nor secrets escape God** (1 Clem 21.3). **Plans** can also be translated *schemes, designs,* or *connivings*.

5

1. Since we know that "God is not to be mocked," we ought to walk in a way worthy of his commandment and glory.

2. Likewise deacons are to be blameless before his righteousness, as servants of God and Christ and not of people. They must not be slanderers or double-tongued, not lovers of money, but self-controlled about everything, compassionate, careful, walking in line with the truth of the Lord, who became a servant of all. And if we would well-please him in the present age, we will also receive the one to come. This is just as he promised us, that he would raise us from the dead and that, if we would conduct ourselves as his worthy citizens, "we will also reign with him"—if, that is, we continue to believe.

5

1. Since "no blemishes escape his notice" (4.3), either in widows or the rest of us, we dare **"not mock God"** (Gal 6:7). Quite possibly the Philippians had previously heard this statement read in church (cf. 3.2). The idea of **walking worthy of his glory** fits well with what Polycarp's disciple Irenaeus will later write, "The **glory** of **God** is the living human being," full of life through "beholding **God**" (Ag Heresies 4.20.7, 3.20.2; 2 Cor 3:18; 1 John 3:2; Rom 6.2). By "the living human being," St. Irenaeus has in mind both individual humans and humanity in Christ. It is "through the good pleasure of the Holy Spirit," that we shall come to this vision of **God**, but not without our part, which is to "be exercised in appropriating to" ourselves "that **glory** that shall hereafter be revealed in those who love **God**" (4.20.8; Rom 8:18–21, 28; Pol 1.2–3). The Christian martyrs show us what "the living human being" looks like (Ag Heresies 5.9.2). Let us **walk**, then, as **we ought**, that we may arrive at that "lasting and unfading **glory**" prepared for us "before the ages" (Eph Sal, 1 Thess 2:12).

2. In a play on words, Polycarp says **the Lord became** the **servant** (in Greek, *deacon*) **of all** and **deacons** are to be **servants** (*deacons*) **of God and Christ**. As with widows (4.3), so now with **deacons**, Polycarp moves from a limited audience to all who may hear his epistle. If we are **blameless before his righteousness** is like **if we well-please him in the present age** (for **Christ** being "**well-pleasing**" to his Father, see Mag 8.2; Matt 3:17, 17:5); and it is like **if we conduct ourselves as his worthy citizens** (for references on this **citizenship**, see Mart Pol 13.2). **If we well-please him** by striving **worthily** in our trials, **we will receive** his **promises** to be **raised from the dead** and "**reign with him**" (2 Tim 2:12). The key to fulfilling our **Lord's** expectations is to **continue to believe**, that is, to keep having our "faith energized through love" more and more all the way to the end (Gal 5:6). This requires a repentance where we never, ever give up, but just keep getting back up.

3. Likewise younger men, too, are to be blameless in every respect, providing for purity above all and reining themselves away from every evil. For it is a beautiful thing to cut oneself off from the lusts in the world, because every lust wages war against the Spirit. "And neither those fornicating with the opposite sex, nor males responding to or initiating sexual relations with males shall inherit the kingdom of God." Nor shall those engaging in worse perversions. Consequently, you must keep away from all these things and freely submit yourselves to the presbyters and deacons as to God and Christ. The virgins are to walk with a blameless and pure conscience.

<h1 style="text-align:center">6</h1>

1. Now as for the presbyters, let them be compassionate, merciful to all, bringing back the ones that have wandered astray, visiting all the sick, not neglecting the widow, orphan, or poor, but always "providing for what is morally beautiful in the sight of God and people." They must refrain from all anger, partiality, and unjust judgment, staying far away from all love of money, neither hastily believing anything against anyone, nor being sharp in judgment, because they know that we all owe the debt of sin.

2. Therefore, if we entreat the Lord to forgive us, we ourselves ought also to forgive. For we are in full view of the eyes of the Lord and of God and must "all stand before the judgment seat of Christ;" and "each one must give an account" of his behavior.

3. In this way, then, "let us serve him with fear and all reverence," just as he himself commanded, and the apostles also, who announced the gospel to us, and the prophets, too, who heralded in advance the coming of our Lord. As men zealous for what is morally beautiful, they used to keep themselves away from the scandalous, from false brothers, and from those who bear the name of the Lord in pretense. Those kinds of people cause the empty-headed to wander astray.

3. **Providing for purity** means taking stock in advance of what will be necessary to hold on to unsullied **purity** and then carrying it out. **Reining** is *guiding by the use of bit and bridle*. **To cut oneself off from** (or *stop short of*) **lusts** is to exert the kind of "violence" that "takes the kingdom by force" (Matt 11:12). **The Spirit** that is **warred against** may be both God's **Spirit** and the human **spirit** (cf. Gal 5:17, 1 Pet 2:11). In addressing **sexual lusts**, Polycarp moves from hetero**sexual** sin to **male** homo**sexual** sin (1 Cor 6:9–10, Eph 16.1) and then to **worse** forms of **sexual perversion**. **The presbyters** may be church *elders* who are *older men* (6.1, Mag 3.1). **Submission to** pastoral oversight and confession of sin is critical when **men** are struggling with **sexual lusts**. The **virgins** are held to the same standard of sexual **purity**.

6

1. Above all, **presbyters** are to **"provide for what is morally beautiful** *before* **God and people"** (Prov 3:4 LXX, Rom 12:17), making spiritual and physical **provision** for their needy flock, in concert with the bishop (Pol 1.2, 2.2). This includes "**bringing back** *those* [like Valens] *who* **have wandered astray**" over the **love of money** (Ezek 34:16, Phil 11.1–4). To avoid the ugliness of **judgmental sin**, all of us must strive **"for what is morally beautiful,"** fully aware **that we all owe the debt of sin** (Matt 6:12, 14–15; 18:21–35; Phil 6.2). **Partiality** (or *respect of persons*) occurs when one *person* is shown more *respect—*or less—than someone else because of position or possessions.

2. Since **we are** always **in full view of** the **Lord and of God**, it behooves us to live like it (Heb 4:13, Isa 1:16–18, 1 Clem 8.4). **"Each one must give an account"** to God (Rom 14:12) **"before Christ's judgment seat"** (Rom 14:10, 2 Cor 5:10) concerning all that we have done and not done (see 6.1 on "the debt of sin that we owe"). Confession is a way that we can come to **Christ** now and set things right before that day.

3. As our **Lord** and Master, Christ **commands us** to **serve him with fear and all reverence** (Ps 2:11, Heb 12:28). **The apostles and prophets** said the same. **They** were fervent **"for what is morally beautiful,"** and "the presbyters" were to be as well (6.1). **To us** could refer to Polycarp hearing the apostles. **The scandalous** are things or people that create a **scandal** (or *stumbling block*), by which people get tripped up (cf. Eph 18.1). **False brothers** teach **falsely**, while **pretenders** (or *hypocrites*) live **falsely**.

DOCETIC PRIDE AND ASCETICAL ENTREATY

7

1. For "everyone who does not confess that Jesus Christ has come in the flesh is an antichrist." And whoever does not confess the testimony of the cross is of the devil. Moreover, whoever twists the sayings of the Lord to suit his own sordid desires and says that there is neither resurrection nor judgment, this man is a firstborn of Satan.

2. Therefore, forsaking the vanity of the masses and their false teachings, let us turn toward the message handed down to us from the beginning, taking the prayers seriously and adhering to fast days, entreating with supplications the all-seeing God "to lead us not into temptation." For as the Lord said, "The spirit is willing, but the flesh is weak."

THE WAY OF THE CROSS

8

1. Let us, then, unceasingly adhere to our hope and to the pledge of our righteousness, which is Christ Jesus. "He bore our sins in his own body upon the tree. He did not commit sin, neither was guile found in his mouth." Instead, for our sakes, that we might live in him, he patiently endured all things.

DOCETIC PRIDE AND ASCETICAL ENTREATY

7

1. The Docetists whom he called "false brothers" (6.3) he now calls "**antichrists**," for "**not confessing that Jesus Christ has come in the flesh**" (1 John 4:2–3, 2 John 7, Sm 5.2) and died on **the cross**. Later Polycarp will call the heretic Marcion "the **firstborn of Satan**" when he meets him in person (Mart Pol Mosc 22.3, Ag Heresies 3.3.4, Sm 4.1, 2 John 10–11).

2. Those who "twist the sayings of the Lord" (7.1) fabricate **false teachings** (cf. Eph 6.2). To not be fooled, we must **turn toward** (or *back to*) **the message** ("the gospel" in 6.3) **handed down** (or *delivered*, here and elsewhere) **to us from the beginning**, which "confesses" that "Jesus has come in the flesh," died on "the cross," and been "resurrected" (7.1). **Taking the message seriously** involves not only what we confess, but also how we conform to the way of life set forth by our **Lord**, one that practices "*almsgiving*" (10.2), **prayer**, and **fasting** (Matt 6:1–18). We should make use of the Church's daily cycle of morning and evening **prayers** (Exod 29:38–39, Ps 118/119:164, Luke 24:52–53, Acts 3:1, Apost Trad 35–36; the Greek in 1 Pet 4:7 and Acts 2:42 reads "**the prayers**"). To **take** these **seriously**, we must *stay focused during* and *act soberly concerning* **the prayers**. Christians **fasted** on Wednesdays and Fridays (Did 8.1) and before Pascha (Ch Hist 5.23.1–2, 5.24.12–13), as the Orthodox Church still does today. **Praying** and **fasting** aid us as we **entreat God** to deliver us from our **weak** and **tempted flesh** (Matt 6:13, 26:41), lest we forsake his "cross" (7.1) and ours (Matt 16:24) and **turn** away from **the Lord**.

THE WAY OF THE CROSS

8

1. "**Adhering to** fast days" (7.2) helps us **adhere to Christ Jesus unceasingly**, and so does **unceasing** prayer (1 Thess 5:17, Pol 1.3, Eph 15.2). By "**bearing our sins upon the tree**," Christ became **our hope and the pledge of our righteousness** (1 Pet 2:24, 22). If we **adhere to him** now, we can "**live righteous lives**" more and more as **we** continue to **live in him** (1 Pet 2:24, Rom 5:17—6:14, Eph 11.1, Mag 5.2).

2. Let us, then, become imitators of his patient endurance; and if we should happen to suffer for his name's sake, let us glorify him. For this is the pattern he clearly sketched for us by his own example, and we ourselves have put our faith in it.

9

1. Therefore, I exhort all of you to obey the message about righteousness and exercise unlimited endurance. Such endurance you also saw with your own eyes, not only in the blessed men Ignatius, Zosimus, and Rufus, but also in others from among you, as well as in Paul himself and the rest of the apostles.

2. Be assured that all these "did not run in vain," but in faith and righteousness. They are in "the place due" to them alongside the Lord, with whom they also suffered. For they "loved" not "the present age," but rather him who died on our behalf and for our sakes was raised by God.

10

1. In these things, therefore, continue to stand fast and keep following the example of the Lord. Be firm and immovable in the faith, lovers of the fellowship of God's family, cherishing each other, joined together in the truth, preferring one another in the gentleness of the Lord, looking down on no one.

2. Christ **"endured** *everything"* for others (8.1); **let us imitate his example** and do the same (1 Pet 2:21). **If suffering for his name should** *occur,* whether or not unto martyrdom, **let us** cheerfully use it to **glorify him** (1 Pet 4:13–16). **His example** of taking up his cross shows us the **pattern.** We are to copy **it** by **faith.**

9

1. **The message** (or *word*) **about righteousness** involves his cross and ours (7.1—8.2). The root for **exercise** refers to *ascetical* **exercise.** By denying himself, Polycarp prepared himself to **endure** martyrdom (for more on *asceticism* and martyrdom, see Mart Pol 18.3). The Philippians had seen this "pattern" of **righteous endurance** "sketched by" the "example" of those who had "suffered [martyrdom] for his name's sake" (8.2, 9.2), including **the blessed Ignatius Zosimus, and Rufus** (on **blessed,** see 1.1), as well as fellow members **from** their own community, St. **Paul himself** (Eph 12.2, 1 Clem 5.1–7), **and** other **apostles.**

2. Just as St. Paul wrote to the Philippians that he had **"not run in vain"** (2:16), so he ended his life sharing in **the Lord's suffering** (or *passion*). **"The place due"** (1 Clem 5.4) comes from a passage regarding the martyrdoms of St. Peter and St. Paul (5.3–7). So martyrs whom "the Lord stood by" (Mart Pol 2.2) are now **alongside the Lord.** In contrast to Demas, who **"loved the present age"** (2 Tim 4:10), **all these** martyrs "adhered to Christ Jesus" (8.1, 7.2).

10

1. **The example of the Lord** provides the "pattern" (8.2) for what Polycarp has been saying (8.1—9.2). On the basis of this **example,** he now sets forth (in 10.1—12.1) how we should live together as witnesses to "the pagans" around us. (Polycarp's exhortations draw on material from Col 1:23, 1 Cor 15:58, 1 Pet 2:17, 1 Pet 3:8, Rom 12:10, and 1 Pet 5:9.) **The faith** may just as easily be translated *faith.* Literally, **fellowship of God's family** is *brotherhood.* The English translations for 10–12, the last sentence of 13, and all of 14 are from Latin translations of the now-lost Greek original.

2. When you can do what is right, do not put it off, "because merciful action delivers from death." "Let all of you freely submit yourselves to one other." "Maintain your conduct above reproach among the pagans," so that you may receive praise "for your good deeds" and the Lord may not be "blasphemed because of you."

3. But woe to the one through whom "the name" of the Lord "is blasphemed." Therefore, teach everyone the sober way in which you also conduct yourselves.

THE FALL AND POSSIBLE RESTORATION OF VALENS

11

1. I am deeply grieved for Valens, who once was made a presbyter among you, that he should so fail to understand the position given to him. Therefore, I admonish you all to avoid the love of money and be pure and truthful. Keep yourselves away from every kind of evil.

2. Moreover, how is someone who cannot control himself in these matters supposed to tell somebody else what to do? If he does not keep himself away from the love of money, he will come to be contaminated by idolatry and be judged as though he were one of the pagans, who fail to understand the judgment of the Lord. Or do we "not know that the saints will judge the world," as Paul teaches?

2. Any "**merciful action** [*almsgiving*] **delivers from death**" (Tob 4:10–11, 12:9–10; Phil 7.2), for, as our Lord said, "Blessed are the **merciful**, for they shall obtain **mercy**" (Matt 5:7). Polycarp also uses other scriptures to encourage **doing what is right** (1 Pet 5:5, 2:12; Isa 52:5 LXX; the latter is also used in Tr 8.2, Rom 2:24, Phil 10.3). These passages emphasize how our voluntary and mutual **submission** (Pol 2.1) can combine with our **irreproachable actions** to elicit **praise** from **pagans**, instead of **blasphemy**.

3. Here Polycarp references Isa 52:5 LXX in a form that is closer to Tr 8.2 than to 10.2 above. A **sober** life is essential (7.2, 11.4; Pol 2.3; Sm 9.1).

THE FALL AND POSSIBLE RESTORATION OF VALENS

11

1. As **a presbyter**, **Valens** had a duty to be attentive to the financial needs of the people and may have been a wealthy man (6.1, 1 Tim 3:3, Titus 1:7–8, 1 Pet 5:2). Prior to addressing the matter of **Valens**, Polycarp mentioned **the love of money** four times (2.2, 4.1, 4.3, 6.1). This section ends with a *warning* to *everyone* not to be proud if **you** do not **love money**, are **pure**, and tell the **truth**. **You** must still *avoid* **every evil** (1 Thess 5:22) and always tell the **truth** about your sins. One way to unhide them is in the reconciling sacrament of confession (see Eph 11.1).

2. Valen's **failure** in **loving money** would have led to **failure** to "provide" for the financial needs of the flock (6.1). He may have even stolen church funds and lied about it (see "truthful" in 11.1). Paul links covetousness, a sin akin to **the love of money** (or *avarice*) with **idolatry** (Col 3:5, Eph 5:5). Just as **pagans will be judged** for their sin of **idolatry**, so unrepentant **lovers of money will come to be judged as pagans** (as was Achan in Joshua 7). It would be far better for our leaders and fellow members to be numbered among **the saints** and "**judge the world**," as **Paul** said (1 Cor 6:2). By saying **we**, Polycarp includes himself.

3. I, however, have not perceived or heard of any such thing among you. It was in your midst that the blessed Paul labored, and you were in his epistles at the beginning. As a matter of fact, he boasts about you in all of the churches that alone at that time knew God. We, however, had not yet come to know him.

4. Therefore, brothers and sisters, I am very grieved for him and for his wife. May the Lord grant them true repentance. You, then, also be clear-headed in this matter, and "do not regard such people as enemies." Rather call them back as hurting and straying members, in order that you may save your entire body. For by doing this, you build yourselves up.

3. **Any such thing** refers to one of them actually "being contaminated by idolatry" (11.2). **Were in his epistles at the beginning** is a translation of a highly problematic Latin translation of the lost Greek original. (For why **epistle** may be plural, see note on 3.2.) **At the beginning** could mean **at the** *start* of the Christian Church, their church, or Paul's ministry. The following alternate translation of the phrase in question ends up with **epistle** in the singular, because of how the Latin case ending is read: *who are addressed at the beginning of his epistle.* Perhaps a few of the original recipients of St. Paul's *Epistle to the Philippians* were still alive when St. Polycarp wrote his **epistle**. In any case, he is **boasting about** the apostolic **beginning** of the church at Philippi in Macedonia—and maybe of the one at Thessalonica, for it was also in Macedonia (see 2 Thess 1:4 on **boasting** and 1 Thess 4:5 on **not knowing God**).

4. Out of personal concern, Polycarp writes **for** twice—**for** Valens and **for his wife. Also** tells the Philippians that not only the straying couple, but they *too,* must **be clear-headed,** *sober-minded* (see Pol 2.3, where Ignatius exhorted Polycarp about this). Polycarp wants his audience to **clearly** see the two as fellow **members** and **"not enemies"** (2 Thess 3:15). **Call them back** (or *restore them*) evokes the image of two who have left (see 6.1). **Save** can also mean *heal, make whole,* or *restore.* In isolation, the souls of individual **members** grow sicker in sin. But together, the **entire body builds** itself **up** in love and each **member** can be *made whole* (3.2, Clem 37.5—38.1, Sm 11.2, 1 Eph 4:16, 1 Tim 4:16, Mart Pol 1.2). In this way, their **entire body may be saved.** Reconciliation and *restoration* reflect true "righteousness" (3.1, 3).

12

1. For I am confident that you are well-trained in the sacred writings and nothing escapes your notice—but to me this has not been granted. Only, as it is said in these scriptures, "Get angry, but do not sin," and "Let not the sun set upon your angriness." Blessed is the one who is mindful of this, which I myself believe to be the case with you.

FINAL PRAYER, INSTRUCTIONS, AND FAREWELL

2. Now may the God and Father of our Lord Jesus Christ, and the eternal High Priest himself, the Son of God, Jesus Christ, build you up in faith and truth, in all gentleness and freedom from anger, in patient endurance, and in long-suffering, tolerance, and purity. And may he grant you a share and a place among his saints, and to us together with you, and to all those under heaven who will come to believe in our Lord and God Jesus Christ and in his Father, who raised him from the dead.

1. Polycarp's entire epistle shows that he is **well-trained in the scriptures**, but, in keeping with Greek rhetoric, he artfully puts himself down (**to me this has not been granted**) so as to exalt his hearers (**which I believe to be the case with you**). He does this so that they may respond righteously to Valens and his wife (11.4). They are permitted to **"get angry"** with the couple, **"but"** must **"not sin"** (Ps 4:5a LXX, Eph 4:26a). The next sentence, starting with **"Let not,"** is found nowhere in the Old Testament. It is a quotation of Eph 4:26b. By referring to both sentences as **these scriptures**, Polycarp is stating that *Ephesians* is just as much **scripture** as *Psalms* is. (1 Tim 5:18, 2 Pet 3:15–16, Barn 4.14, and 2 Clem 2.4 also refer to various New Testament texts as **scripture**.) With St. Polycarp, the contours of the New Testament canon are becoming clearer: one way or another he utilizes every New Testament book but *Philemon, Third John,* and *Revelation.* His disciple St. Irenaeus additionally uses *Revelation,* citing it extensively. More importantly, however, he clearly establishes that only *The Gospels of Matthew, Mark, Luke,* and *John* are apostolic and authoritative for the Church (*Ag Heresies* 3.11.7–9). We know that Polycarp will be sending them Ignatius's *Epistle to the Ephesians* along with this epistle (13.2). Polycarp's phrase, **"Nothing escapes your notice,"** is almost identical to Ignatius's, **"None of these things escapes your notice"** (Eph 14.1, 15.3; Phil 4.3). Both phrases are located in passages that stress the importance of preserving Christian community and matching our deeds to our faith and love (compare Phil 11.3—12.1 with Eph 13.1—14.2). Apparently, Polycarp wants his audience to apply Ignatius's epistle to their situation.

FINAL PRAYER, INSTRUCTIONS, AND FAREWELL

2. We share with **God** the **Father** and our **High Priest Jesus Christ** the duty of **building** ourselves **up** as **Christ's** Body (11.4, 1 Cor 14:12, Jude 20; for **Christ** as **High Priest**, see Mart Pol 14.3; Phld 9.1; Heb 4:14, 7:3). The **saints** are the departed who are alive with **Christ**. The manuscript evidence and translators are evenly split on whether to include **and God** between **our Lord** and **Jesus Christ**. Polycarp has great confidence in the future spread of the gospel **to all those under heaven who will come to believe**.

3. Pray for all the saints. Pray, too, for kings, magistrates, and rulers, as well as for those who persecute and hate you and for the enemies of the cross. By this, your fruit may be evident among all, so that you may be perfect in him.

13

1. Both you and Ignatius wrote to me that if anyone happens to be leaving for Syria, he should also take along your letter. This is the very thing I will do if I can get a suitable opportunity, whether I do it myself or do it through the man I will send as an envoy to act for both of us.

3. **All the saints** is best understood to include **all the** faithful, both living and departed. Thus we **pray for all** who now believe and "will come to believe," as well as for **all** the departed who await the fulfillment of their lot when they "share in the resurrection" (Phil 12.2, Mart Pol 14.2). When the Latin or Greek is translated **among all**, it refers to people; when it is rendered *in everything*, it refer to circumstances. **Enemies of the cross**, a phrase Paul used (Phil 3:18), probably refers to the Jews (7.1; Phil 3:1–3; Mart Pol 12.2, 13.1, 17.2, 18.1). **Prayers for** our oppressors make **evident** our **fruitful** love and **perfect** us **in him** (Matt 5:43–48, Luke 6:27–28, Jas 1:4). No love, no **fruit**, no **perfection** (see comments on Eph 2.2). Roman emperors traveling in the east were hailed as *basileus* (Greek for **king**), though none in Rome was ever called *rex* (Latin for **king**).That was unthinkable, since the Romans had rid themselves of **kings** to establish their republic. Even when Constantinople fell in 1453, her citizens still sang of themselves as being a "commonwealth" (that is, a *republic*) in the *Troparion Hymn for the Elevation of the Precious and Life-Giving Cross.*

13

1. Based on what Polycarp writes here and in 13.2, it seems that his *Epistle to the Philippians* was written before he had all the details of **Ignatius's** martyrdom, and thus some forty years before his own martyrdom (Pol 7.1—8.1, Phil 9.1, Mart Pol 21.1, Rom 10.3 with comments). From the fact that the church at Philippi is **sending** a **letter** to the church at Antioch in **Syria**, it is evident that the Philippians know of the "peace" that has come to their sister church and that they are writing to "congratulate them" (Phld 10.1–2, Sm 11.1–3, Pol 7.1—8.2).

2. We are sending to you, as you directed, the epistles of Ignatius, the ones sent to us by him and as many others as we have with us. They are appended to this epistle. From them you will be able to draw great benefit, for they cover faith, endurance, and every edifying matter that involves our Lord. Also, about Ignatius himself and about those with him, notify us of anything more definite that you may have come to know.

14

1. I have written this to you through Crescens. I commended him to you recently and now commend him again. For while he was with us he conducted himself blamelessly, and I believe he will act the same way with you. Moreover, you shall consider his sister to be commended when she comes to you. May you fare well in the Lord Jesus Christ in grace, along with all who are yours. Amen.

2. Polycarp is forwarding to the Philippians all **the epistles of Ignatius** that he has. These include *Smyrnaeans* and *Polycarp*, which **Ignatius sent to** him. In all likelihood, they also include *Ephesians* (Eph 21.1, Phil 12.1), *Magnesians* (Mag 15.1), and *Trallians* (Tr 12.1), all of which were sent *from* Smyrna, as well as *Philadelphians*, which was sent *from* Troas (Phld 11.2). Scholars think that Polycarp probably did not have *Romans* (though we know from Rom 10.1 that it was also sent *from* Smyrna), because the history of that epistle's manuscript transmission was separate from that of the others. Polycarp's estimation of **Ignatius's epistles** is heartfelt, pious, and instructive: by them we can grow in our personal **faith in our Lord**, learn to more **patiently endure for our Lord**, and be **edified** (be *built up*; 3.2, 11.4, 12.2) by **every matter that involves our Lord**. **Also**, Polycarp wants them to update him on anything they **may know** about the martyrdoms of **Ignatius and** his companions.

14

1. **Through Crescens** could indicate that he was Polycarp's amanuensis, letter-bearer, or both. The Latin word translated **recently** usually means *at present*. Some have translated it *in person*, indicating a close relationship between Polycarp and the Philippian church. What integrity and trustworthiness **Crescens** possesses: **his conduct** is so **blameless** that he remains **commendable** over time. And for him to also have such a **commendable sister** speaks **well** of their parents. We **fare well in the Lord Jesus Christ** when we abide **in grace** and behave **blamelessly** (Eph 10.3, 8.2, 20.2).

The Martyrdom of St. Polycarp

CONTENTS

SALUTATION

The church of God sojourning at Smyrna to the church of God sojourning in Philomelium and to all the communities of the Holy and Catholic Church sojourning in every place. May mercy, peace, and love from God the Father and our Lord Jesus Christ be multiplied.

MARTYRDOM IN ACCORDANCE WITH THE GOSPEL

1

1. We write to you, brothers and sisters, of the events concerning those who bore witness by being martyred, especially the blessed Polycarp. He put an end to the persecution by sealing it, so to speak, with his martyrdom. For nearly everything that previously occurred took place that the Lord might show us again a martyrdom that is in accordance with the gospel.

2. For he waited to be handed over, just as the Lord also had, that we ourselves might also become imitators of him, "not only looking out for our" own "interests, but also for those of" our neighbors. For it is characteristic of true and firm love not only to desire oneself to be saved, but all the brothers and sisters as well.

SALUTATION

Here is the first of the author's four references to **the Catholic Church** (for the other three, see 8.1, 16.2, 19.2; for the first written instance of the term **Catholic Church**, which was penned by Ignatius, see Sm 8.2). Our **sojourning** takes place **in communities** (see Phil Sal; 1 Clem Sal; Mag 13.2, 1.2). In fact, the English word *parishes* comes from the Greek word for **sojourning communities**. **Philomelium** was a city of Phrygia located inside the eastern border of the province of Asia between **Smyrna** to the west and Antioch to the east. Phrygia had a reputation for being timid. An example of this is Quintus's "cowardice" (in 4.1). In the late second century, Phrygia became known for Montanism, a rigorist, charismatic movement among Christians that became a heretical sect.

MARTYRDOM IN ACCORDANCE WITH THE GOSPEL

1

1. **Those who bore witness by being martyred** can also be translated *those who were martyred* (21.1, 22.1; Tr 12.3). **Bearing witness** to and **being martyred** for Jesus Christ went together for St. Paul (Acts 22:12-22). Here **blessed** is synonymous with *saint* (see Phil 3.2). A **seal** indicated that a transaction was finished. (On another bishop's **martyrdom putting an end to persecution**, see comments on Phld 10.1 about Ignatius.) **Again** and *from above* are different translations of the same word, which can have both meanings at the same time (John 3:3-7). **The Lord shows** his providence in overseeing *from above* the details of **Polycarp's martyrdom**. At the same time, he **shows again** a **martyrdom that is in accordance with the gospel**, one which is like his own (1.2, 2.1, 19.1).

2. Why is Polycarp's martyrdom said to be "in accordance with the gospel" (1.1)? *Because* **he waited to be handed over, just as the Lord also had** (cf. 4.1), **that we might become imitators of him. Him** refers primarily to Polycarp, but also calls to mind **the Lord**. Christ provides "the pattern" for **imitation** (Phil 8.2), Polycarp the immediate example to **imitate**. He is the model **martyr** who accepts death in **imitation of** his **Lord**. With **true and firm love** he **"looks out for those"** around him (Phil 2:4), **desiring** that they **all be saved** (Phil 2:1-13, Eph 10.3, Pol 1.2, Phil 11.4). Even when our suffering is not unto death, our lives should still embody these **loving concerns**.

2

1. Blessed and noble, therefore, are all the martyrdoms that have taken place in accordance with the will of God (for we, on account of being very pious, ought to ascribe to God the absolute power over all).

2. For who would not marvel at their brave nobility and their display of endurance and love for the Master? Some with patience endured, being torn to shreds with whips to the point that the fabric of their flesh was exposed down to the veins and arteries within. As a consequence, even the bystanders felt pity and lamented. Others reached such a height of nobility that not one of them uttered a cry or a groan, demonstrating to absolutely all of us that, at the very hour in which they were being tortured, the noble martyrs of Christ were leaving behind their flesh—or what is greater, the Lord was standing by and conversing with them.

2

1. The **noble** (and *brave*) character of **martyrs** (described here and in 2.2) is first recorded in the archetypal **martyrdoms** of Eleazar and the mother with her seven sons, who died as Jewish martyrs under Antiochus IV Epiphanes (2 Macc 6:18–20, 27–31; 7:1–2, 5, 10–11, 20–21; 4 Macc 6:5, 10, 22; 8:3; 16:16; 17:11–24). The elderly Eleazar is described as "a **noble** athlete" who "triumphed over his torturers as he was being beaten" (4 Macc 6:10, Pol 3.1). **Noble** is also used of Christian **martyrs** (specifically St. Peter and St. Paul in 1 Clem 5.1, 6). Because **absolute power over all** *persons and* **all** *things* belongs **to God**, the choice should be his whether our *witness* ends in physical death, that is, in **martyrdom**. So did he choose for the **martyrs** mentioned in this account (2.2–4, 3.1–2, 19.1–2), but not so for Quintus (4.1).

2. Because of **their brave nobility, endurance**, and **love for** their **Master**, even **the bystanders lamented** their **torture** (cf. 3 Macc 4:3–4). Literally, **torn to shreds** is *carded* (like wool). The Greek for **leaving behind** includes the idea of *going abroad*, and thus, in this case, points to *leaving for* their heavenly *home*. **The martyrs demonstrate** that the *witness* of Christians, whether or not unto death, is only successful **at their hour** of trial when they **leave behind** their **flesh**—by dying to it—to commune **with the Lord**. He, in turn, comes to **stand by them at** that **hour** and strengthen **them** with his words (cf. 2 Tim 4:17). Most of us will not end our earthly lives in **martyrdom**, but all of us are called to bear our crosses with **martyric** valor to the crucifixion of our **fleshly** passions (Gal 2:20, 5:24, 6:14; regarding Germanicus, see 3.3).

3. And fixing their attention on the grace of Christ, they were scorning the torments of this world and by a single hour were redeeming themselves from eternal punishment. In fact, the fire of their inhuman torturers felt cold to them, for what they kept setting before their eyes was escaping from the eternal and never-extinguished fire. And so with the eyes of the heart they kept looking up to the good things reserved for those who patiently endure: "things which neither ear has heard, nor eye seen, nor have entered into the human heart." Now this was beginning to be shown to them by the Lord, for these people were no longer human beings, but already angels.

4. And likewise also the ones condemned to the wild beasts endured dreadful punishments. They were forced to lie down on sharp seashells and were afflicted with a variety of other kinds of tortures. This was done in order that, if it were possible, the afflicter might bend them to denial through their relentless punishment.

3

1. Many, indeed, were the devices the devil was using against them. But, thanks be to God, he failed to prevail against everyone. For the most noble Germanicus turned their cowardice into courage through the patient endurance that was in him. Indeed, he fought the wild beasts with outstanding valor. For when the proconsul wished to persuade him and told him to have pity on his age, he forcibly pulled the wild beast upon himself, wishing a quick release from their unrighteous and lawless life.

3. The phrase **fixing their attention on** can be rendered *giving heed to*. **Redeeming themselves** may be translated *winning their freedom*. "The hour" of their martyrdom (2.2) becomes the **hour** of their **redemption** (2.3). **Christ,** "in whom we have **redemption**" (Col 1:14), rewards them with **eternal** life for their **single hour** of combat for him. Polycarp himself later speaks to the proconsul of the "**fire** that burns but **an hour**" and "**the fire** of **eternal punishment**" (Mart Pol 11.2). **Endure** refers specifically to making it through **the hour** of **the fire**. The clause that begins with **those things which neither ear has heard** and ends with **the human heart** may draw on—but not be a verbatim quote of—several different sources (Isa 64:4/64:3 OSB, 65:16–17; 1 Cor 2:9; 1 Clem 34.8; pagan and Christian authors were not so particular about quoting verbatim as we moderns are). **Entered into the heart** (like *come to mind*) refers to all that any of us could ever conceive of what "God has prepared for those who love him" (I Cor 2:9). Those being martyred have **already** become **angelic,** beholding the face of God and viewing **the good things reserved** for them in heaven (cf. Matt 18:10, 22:30; Luke 20:34–37; also see Stephen in Acts 6:15, 7:55–56).

4. The kind of **seashells** referred to are marine gastropod mollusks. Because of their **sharp** spire, they were broken and placed atop walls for security against intruders. The Romans frequently used them in **torturing** Christians before they martyred them. Literally, **the afflicter** is *he* and refers to "the devil," who is named in the next sentence (3.1).

3

1. **The devil** was the one actively lurking behind the **many devices of torture.** We will see **the devil prevail against** Quintus (4.1), **but** he did not **prevail against everyone** (2.1—3.1). **Their cowardice** means the *fearfulness* of the Christians. Germanicus was able to transform this *fear* by **the patient endurance that was in him,** that had become part of **him,** through the cultivation of **patience** (2 Pet 1:4-11, especially verses 5–6 and 10–11). The **proconsul** is Lucius Statius Quadratus (21.1). He is governor of the Roman province of Asia and resides in Ephesus, its capital. **Age** refers to Germanicus's *youth* (in 9.2 it has reference to Polycarp's *old* "**age**"). **Germanicus** acts "**forcibly,**" as Ignatius had said he himself would (Rom 5.2). By so doing, he is **released from their** oppressive **unrighteous and lawless life,** as well as his own physical **life,** and thus exchanges these for eternal **life.**

2. Consequently, after this, all of the crowd—despite their marveling at the brave nobility of the God-loving and God-fearing race of the Christians—began to cry out, "Away with the atheists! Find Polycarp!"

4

1. But one named Quintus, a Phrygian recently arrived from Phrygia, grew cowardly when he saw the wild beasts. Now this was the man who had pressured himself, and some others as well, to come forward voluntarily. After making many appeals, the proconsul persuaded him to swear and offer incense. Therefore, brothers and sisters, on account of this we do not praise those who hand themselves over, since the gospel does not teach us to act that way.

POLYCARP'S WITHDRAWAL, ARREST, AND TRANSPORT

5

1. Now the most marvelous Polycarp, when he first heard, was not disturbed, but wanted to remain in town. But the majority persuaded him to withdraw quietly, so he went away to a house in the country not far from the city. He was staying there with a few people, doing nothing else night and day but praying for everybody and for the churches throughout the inhabited world, for this was his regular habit.

2. Second-century **Christians** referred to themselves as a **race** separate from Jews and Gentiles (Diogn 1; Mart Pol 14.1, 17.1). Earlier St. Peter had called **Christians** "a chosen **race**" and "a holy nation" (1 Pet 2:9). The expression "holy nation" was first used of the Jews (Exod 19:5–6), but Christ told them this would soon change because they had rejected him: "The kingdom of God shall be taken away from you and given to a nation producing its fruits" (Matt 21:43, 33–46). Although **the crowd** may **marvel at the bravery of the Christians**, they still denounce them as **atheists** (cf. 9.2, Tr 3.2) because they do not worship their gods, who hold together the pagan social order of Rome and Smyrna. Like **with** Jesus and Paul (Luke 23:18 and Acts 21:36), they **cry out, "Away with Polycarp!"**

4

1. The author is contrasting the example of **Quintus** (4.1) with that of Germanicus (3.1) as a prelude to the story of Polycarp (starting at 5.1). The Christians in Philomelium, to whom *The Martyrdom of Polycarp* was addressed, may have heard of **Quintus** since he came from **Phrygia** where they lived (Sal). The newcomer first **pressures himself and others to come forward**, then **grows cowardly when he sees the wild beasts**, and finally **swears** an oath to the emperor and **offers** him **incense**. But Germanicus, when called upon to die, turned the "**cowardice**" of **others** "into courage" and "forced the wild beast upon himself" (3.1). Martyrdom **volunteered** for under **pressure** should **not** be **praised**, lest it fail to be "in accordance with **the gospel**" (1.1, 1.2, 20.1). The case of bishops, however, can be different (see comments on Phld 10.1 concerning St. Ignatius).

POLYCARP'S WITHDRAWAL, ARREST, AND TRANSPORT

5

1. What **Polycarp first heard** was "the crowd crying out, 'Away with the atheists! Find **Polycarp!**'" (3.2). That he was not **disturbed** by this shows how **marvelous** a man he was. He did **not** seek out martyrdom; nor did he try to escape it. He would not have **departed** had not **the majority** insisted, but he did **not go far. Everybody** he **prayed for** included those who wanted him dead (for **Polycarp's** relevant statements on forgiveness and **prayer**, see Phil 12.1–3). **He** was not afraid, but just kept on doing what **he regularly** did.

2. And while he was praying, he had a vision that before three days he would be arrested, and he saw his pillow burning with fire. Then he turned and said to those with him, "I must be burned alive."

6

1. And because those searching for him persisted, he moved to another country house. Then, right after he left, those searching for him showed up. And when they did not find him, they arrested two young slaves, the second of whom confessed under torture.

2. For it was quite impossible for him to remain hidden, since the very ones who betrayed him were members of his own household. And the irenarch (whose lot it was to be called by the same name as Herod) was hurrying to bring him into the stadium, in order that he might fulfill his own lot of becoming a partaker of Christ, while those who betrayed him might undergo the punishment of Judas himself.

2. The fulfillment of this **vision** will occur when Polycarp's body is engulfed in **burning fire** without, however, him being **burned** to death (12.3, 15.1—16.1). The Romans had one plan, the Lord another. It is only after his death that his body is **burned** to ashes (18.1).

6

1. **Those** that **showed up right afterward** came to the first **house**. Since the **two slaves** were "members of his own household" (6.2), St. Polycarp appears to have been a wealthy patron to his flock (see Life Pol 3–5 on his inheriting a large estate from the lady who bought his freedom). The churches regulated the treatment of **slaves** in Christian households, but did not forbid owning them (Eph 6:5–9, Col 3:22—4:1, 1 Tim 6:1–2, Titus 2:9–10, 1 Cor 7:20–21, Phlm 8–21, Pol 4.3).

2. **Polycarp**, like **Christ**, is **betrayed** by one **of his own**, who "confessed" **his** location (6.1, John 18:1–3). **Irenarchs** were public servants in charge of keeping the peace at personal cost. **Herod** was a common Greek **name** with powerful associations for Christians. **Herod** the Great tried to kill **Christ** (Matt 2:1–23). His son, **Herod** Antipas, had John the Baptist beheaded (Matt 14:1–12) and was complicit in **Christ's** crucifixion (Luke 23:6–12, Acts 4:27, Sm 1.2). The irenarch tries by **hurrying to** better **his own lot** in this life, but God "*from above*" (1:1) uses him to **fulfill** Polycarp's **lot of becoming a partaker of Christ**. (For more contrasts between man's evil intent and God's blessed conclusion, see John 11:47–53 about **Christ**, Gen 50:20 about Joseph, and Eph 19.3 about humanity.) The area in the **stadium** where the martyrs contested was the arena.

7

1. So on Friday, about the time of the evening meal, mounted police and horsemen, with the young slave in tow, set out armed with their usual weapons as though advancing upon a bandit. And having closed in on him at a late hour, they found him in a certain cottage lying down in an upper room. Now from there he could have gotten away to another place in the country, but he refused, saying, "God's will be done."

2. So when he heard that they had arrived, he came down and talked with them. Those present marveled at his age and composure, and wondered why there was so much bother over the arrest of such an elderly man. Then at once he ordered that all the food and drink they might desire be set before them at that hour. And he asked them to give him an hour to pray undisturbed.

3. Now when they consented, he stood and prayed. And he was so full of the grace of God that for two hours he could not keep silent. Those listening were amazed, and many regretted that they had come after such a right godly old man.

1. The word used here for **Friday**—and still employed by Greeks today for the sixth day of the week—is *Preparation*. It refers to the day of Christ's passion, which occurred on a **Friday** (John 19:31). Other connections to Christ and his passion include men **armed** with **weapons** coming to arrest him (Matt 26:47, John 18:3), and mention of a **bandit** (or *robber*; John 18:40; Matt 26:55, 27:38), **an upper room** (Mark 14:15, Acts 1:13), a **meal** with "betrayal" by "one of" his own (Matt 26:21–25 with 6.1–2), and verbal acceptance of **God's "will"** (Matt 26:39–44). Presumably, **the young slave** was the one who "confessed under torture" (6.1).

2. **Marveled** and **wondered** translate the same word. **His age and composure** set them at ease as to any danger they might be in, but also made them question **why** there needed to be **so much bother** (literally, *haste*) about his **arrest**. So when **he** extended hospitality to his enemies, they were willing to take time for **food and drink** and let him **pray undisturbed** "for two hours" (6.3). Ironically, the prisoner is the one in charge.

3. **Right godly** depicts Polycarp as an **old** (or *elderly*) **man** to whom it is **right** (or *proper*) to show the same respect as one shows to **God** (about his age, see the Introduction to St. Polycarp). Perhaps this is why his captors let him **pray** for twice as long as he asked (7.2). After the word **prayed**, a variant reading adds, "facing east (or facing *the sunrise*)." **Standing** facing east is the standard orientation of Orthodox churches, worship, and personal prayer. To **pray** facing *the sunrise* is to **pray** to *the risen* Christ, "*the Sun* of Righteousness" (Mal 4:2), who will return from the east (Matt 24:27).

8

1. Now when at last he had finished his prayer, having remembered every single person who had ever even come in contact with him, both small and great, illustrious and obscure, and the entire Catholic Church throughout the inhabited world, the hour came for his departure. So they sat him upon an ass and brought him into the city. It was a special Sabbath.

2. And the irenarch Herod and his father Nicetes met Polycarp and transferred him onto their carriage. They were sitting beside him, trying to persuade him, even saying, "Why, what harm is there in saying, 'Caesar is Lord,' and offering incense" (and other words such as these), "so that you save yourself?" Now at first he did not answer them, but when they kept persisting, he said, "I am not about to do what you advise me."

3. So, after failing to persuade him, they began making threats and made him get down from the carriage in such a hurry that he bruised his shin as he descended. And without even turning around, acting as if he had suffered nothing, he hurried along eagerly as he was being led into the stadium. Now there was such an uproar inside the stadium that nobody could even be heard.

8

1. Since Polycarp **remembered every single person** he **had ever** met, it is reasonable to expect he **prayed** not only for the living, but also for the departed, a practice Christians received from the Jews (2 Macc 12:38–45, 15:12–16; 2 Tim 1:16–18). **The hour, an ass,** his **departure,** and **a special** (literally, *great*) **Sabbath** remind us of our Lord's journey to his passion (John 17:1, 12:23, 12:14–15, 13:1, 19:31). While there is no consensus on what **a special Sabbath** was, the events surrounding Polycarp's martyrdom do appear to take place during a festival, over which Phillip the Asiarch has come from Tralles to preside (Mart Pol 12.2, 21.1; on the martyrdom of St. Pionius on **a special Sabbath,** see Mart Pion 2.1, 3.6). The major Jewish feasts were called **Sabbaths** (Lev 23:1–3), though they rarely occurred on a Saturday. The linking of feast and **Sabbath** may have given rise at Smyrna to the Jews using the term **special Sabbath** for a **Sabbath** coinciding with a civic holiday. Both Polycarp's martyrdom and Pionius's later arrest at Smyrna occurred on February 23, which happened to be a Saturday **Sabbath** and the very day of the celebration of the feast of *Terminalia,* when the last day of the old Roman year was commemorated (21.1, Mart Pion 2.1).

2. **Herod and Nicetes** are pressuring **Polycarp** from both **sides.** Silent **at first,** he finally makes clear **he** will **not offer incense.** Rather than "save his life," he "will lose it" "for the sake of" the **Lord** (Matt 16:25). To call **Caesar Lord** and **offer** him **incense** would be to commit idolatry and deny that Jesus Christ is **Lord** (cf. Matt 10:32–33, 16:24).

3. Polycarp remains in charge. **Nothing** will deter him from his martyrdom. **Persuasion fails, threats fail, bruising his shin fails.** They move against **him hurriedly.** He, in turn, **hurries along eagerly into the stadium.** While all this is going on, in anticipation of his arrival, the crowd of spectators **in the stadium** is already in **an uproar.**

POLYCARP'S CONFESSION IN THE STADIUM

9

1. But as Polycarp was entering into the stadium, a voice came from heaven, "'Be strong,' Polycarp, 'and act like a man.'" And no one saw who spoke, but those of our people who were present heard the voice. And when he was finally led forward, a great uproar arose from those who had heard that Polycarp had been arrested.

2. So when he had been brought forward, the proconsul asked him whether he was Polycarp. And when he confessed, he tried to persuade him to recant saying, "Respect your age," and other such things as they used to say: "Swear by the genius of Caesar." "Repent!" "Say, 'Away with the atheists!'" But Polycarp, with a stern expression on his face, looked at the entire crowd of lawless pagans in the stadium and pointed toward them with his hand. Then groaning and looking up to heaven, he said, "Away with the atheists!"

3. But when the proconsul was insistent and said, "Swear, and I will release you. Revile Christ," Polycarp said, "For eighty-six years I have been serving him and he has done me no wrong. How can I possibly blaspheme my King, who saved me?"

POLYCARP'S CONFESSION IN THE STADIUM

9

1. Despite the deafening "uproar" (8.3), **Polycarp** and the Christians **heard from heaven** what Joshua had **heard: "'Be strong and act like a man'"** (Josh 1:6 LXX). All that the crowd **heard**, however, was **that Polycarp had been arrested. When he** walked **forward**, their earlier "uproar" (8.3) erupted into **a great uproar.**

2. Here **Polycarp** likely made the same **confession** he will soon make again: "I am a Christian" (10.1). His being a Christian is what **the proconsul** wanted him to **recant** (or *deny*). Ironically, **the proconsul** told **Polycarp** to **repent** (*change his mind*) and repudiate the Christians as **atheists. But Polycarp pointed toward the lawless pagans** and said of **them, "Away with the atheists!"** (For which groups are called **atheists** in the texts of St. Ignatius and St. Polycarp, see Tr 3.2, Tr 10.1, and Mart Pol 3.2.) **The genius** (literally, *good fortune*) **of Caesar** is said to be his family's creative, guardian spirit, which has been elevated to the level of divinity and is expected to ensure *good fortune* for the Empire.

3. It looks as though **eighty-six years** is **Polycarp's** age (but see the Introduction to St. Polycarp for a very different view). If this was his age, as the majority of scholars suppose, this would suggest that he saw himself as **saved** when he was baptized as an infant and **served Christ** from that time on. This would place his birth around the year 69, based on a date for his martyrdom of 155 (21.1). It was the custom of the Jews to baptize male Gentile converts with their entire households, including infant children. The apostles continued this practice of baptizing households (Acts 16:15, 31–34; 1 Cor 1:16). **Serving him** can also be translated *his slave* (see Phil 2.1). In declaring that **Christ** is his **King, Polycarp** is confessing that he is a Christian and proclaiming that Caesar has no final right to rule over him. Better it is for him to **revile** "Caesar," by refusing to "**swear** by" his "genius" (9.2, 10.1), than to **blaspheme Christ**, his **King** and **Savior.** When Roman emperors were in the eastern part of the empire, people often called them "**kings**" (Phil 12.3).

10

1. But when he insisted yet again and said, "Swear by the genius of Caesar," he replied, "If you vainly suppose that I will swear by your so-called genius of Caesar, and are pretending not to know me, not to know who I am, listen clearly: I am a Christian. If, however, you want to learn what Christianity teaches, set a day and give me a hearing."

2. The proconsul said, "Persuade the people." Then Polycarp responded, "You at least I counted worthy of a reasoned reply. For we have been taught to show honor to rulers and authorities instituted by God, which is proper so long as it does us no harm. But as for those people, I do not regard them as worthy of my making a defense before them."

11

1. And the proconsul said, "I have wild beasts. I will throw you to them, unless you repent." But he said, "Call them. For the change we cannot make is repentance from better to worse, but it is virtuous to change from hard-hearted deeds to acts of justice."

2. And again he spoke to him, "I shall have you consumed by fire if you continue to scorn the wild beasts, unless you repent." But Polycarp replied, "You threaten with fire that burns but an hour and is soon put out. For you do not know the fire of the coming judgment and eternal punishment, which is reserved for the impious. But why are you hesitating? Bring on what you will."

10

1. In their exchange, Polycarp is making **clear** what was implied earlier on (in 9.2), that the proconsul would like to avoid putting the old man to death. But Polycarp refuses to let him off so easily. He **clearly** (or *openly in public*) affirms that he is **a Christian**, and taunts the proconsul to **listen** to him *with openness, with an open mind*. To Roman officials, **set a day and give me a hearing** would mean *grant me a trial*. To avoid Polycarp's execution, **however**, the proconsul cannot allow this.

2. Not wanting to be responsible for **Polycarp's** death, **the proconsul** directs him to **persuade the people**. The bloodthirsty crowd, however, was **not worthy** of **a reasoned reply** because their passion-controlled minds were incapable of receiving such **a defense** (cf. Matt 7:6). **A reasoned reply** and **a defense** would utilize "what Christianity teaches" (10.1). The **harm** that the saint has in mind is the **harm** that comes to the soul of anyone who violates his conscience by **improper** obedience to any **authority** that is acting contrary to **God** (Acts 5:27–29).

11

1. Note how **the proconsul** perverts true **repentance** (**changing** *one's mind*) into a **change** for the **worse** (cf. 9.2, 11.2). Consider the contrast between the **hard heart** that **the proconsul** is about to exhibit and the **just** character that Polycarp has always shown (17.1; cf. Phil 4.1, which appears to have the presbyter Valens in mind). Note also that the Romans prided themselves on their administration of **justice**. Polycarp uses the opportunity afforded by **the proconsul's** own words—**"you repent"**—to preach the gospel and give "a reasoned reply" (10.2).

2. One of the teachings of the Christian faith that **Polycarp** is confessing to the proconsul is our firm belief in **the final judgment**. While the proconsul is quick to **threaten, Polycarp** does not fear **the** earthly "**fire**" that he **knows** is **coming** for him (5.2). He realizes that the proconsul has actually been **hesitating** all along over executing him. He confronts the proconsul about this by challenging him: **"Bring on what you will."**

12

1. Now as he was saying these and many other words, he was being filled full of courage and joy, and his face was being filled with grace. As a result, not only did his countenance not drop in dismay at what was said to him, but, on the contrary, the proconsul was beside himself and ended up sending his own herald into the midst of the stadium to announce, "Three times Polycarp has confessed he is a Christian."

2. When this had been proclaimed by the herald, the entire crowd—made up of both pagans and Jews residing in Smyrna—began roaring in uncontrollable rage with a loud voice, "This one is the teacher of impiety, the father of the Christians, the destroyer of our gods, the one who teaches many not to sacrifice or worship!" As they were making these exclamations, they started roaring for Philip the Asiarch to let loose a lion upon Polycarp. But he said he could not legally do so, since he had already ended the wild-beast games.

3. Then it seemed good to them to cry out in unison that he burn Polycarp alive. For it was necessary that the vision that had appeared to him about his pillow be fulfilled, when he saw it on fire while he was praying and had turned and said prophetically to the faithful around him, "I must be burned alive."

12

1. As Polycarp's mouth **was saying many words**, his heart was **being filled** to the brim with **courage and joy** (Matt 10:18–20), and so **his countenance did not drop** (cf. Prov 15:13/15:14 OSB). Three times Polycarp had confessed Christ (9.2, 9.3, 10.1; cf. 1 Tim 6:12–13). He had also refused to say, "'Caesar is Lord,' "offer incense," and "save" himself (8.2). Neither had he "recanted" (9.2), "sworn by the genius of Caesar" (9.2, 9.3, 10.1), or "repented" (9.2, 11.1, 11.2). And he had not "reviled Christ" or "blasphemed" him either (9.3; compare this with Peter's **threefold** denial and **confession** in John 18:15–27, 21:15–17.) After **three confessions**, the Romans would proceed to execution.

2. Two manuscripts read *teacher of Asia* for **teacher of impiety** (as does Eusebius: see Polycarp Intro, 157, fn. 1). The ultimate **impiety** to *Gentiles* **and Jews** was Polycarp's calling Christ "King" (9.3). So with one voice the two groups raised an "uproar" (8.3, 9.1, 12.3; cf. Acts 14:4–6, 17:5–8), though the words they **roared** may not have all been the same. **Philip** was provincial high priest in **Asia** over the cult of Rome and the emperor (21.1). He was using his earlier **ending** of **the wild-beast games** as a **legal** excuse to avoid responsibility for **Polycarp's** death in an attempt to blame **the crowd** (or *multitude*). Yet the proconsul had just threatened Polycarp with these very **beasts** (11.1–2)! Pilate had acted the same way when he blamed the **Jews** for Jesus's death (Matt 27:24–25). **The wild-beast** (or *hunting*) **games** included a variety of competitions involving men and animals in the arena. Condemned criminals like Ignatius and Polycarp were an expendable group brought out to gorge the bloodlust of **the crowd**.

3. It was "the crowd" (13.1), not the proconsul, that decided **Polycarp** should die. Of the methods of execution used by the Romans, only crucifixion was worse than **being burned alive**. By **prophesying** his coming death, **Polycarp** followed the pattern set by Jesus. Yet **Polycarp** only knew and **prophesied** "in part" (1 Cor 13:9, 12), for in God's mercy his body was not **burned** until after his death (5.2, 13.3, 15.1—16.1, 18.1, 16.2). Jesus, however, knew and **prophesied** completely his own death on the cross (John 3:14, 12:32–33).

POLYCARP'S MARTYRDOM

13

1. Then what followed happened very quickly—in less time than it takes to tell. All of a sudden the crowd was gathering up wood and kindling from both the workshops and baths, especially the Jews, who were assisting in these actions with their usual zeal.

2. Now when the combustible material for the funeral pyre was ready, he took off all his outer clothing by himself and removed his undergarment. He also tried to unlatch his sandals, though previously he was not in the habit of doing so, because each one of the faithful was always hurrying to be the first to touch his bare skin. For he had been treated with honor in every respect on account of his godly citizenship, even before his martyrdom.

3. So right away the materials collected for the funeral pyre were placed around him. But as they were just about to nail him, he said, "Leave me as I am, for he who grants me to endure the fire will grant me to remain on the funeral pyre unmoved without the security of your nails."

POLYCARP'S MARTYRDOM

13

1. The author seems quite eager to single out **the Jews** for their continual **assistance in** such **actions** (cf. 17.2). But is it credible that they were **gathering up wood** on "a Sabbath" (8.1, 21.1; Num 15:32–36) and that they were part of **the crowd** in the stadium on such a day (see 12.2–3)? Yet St. John had said those in Smyrna who called themselves **Jews** were really "a synagogue of Satan" (Rev 2:8–9, Phld 6.1). After the **Jewish** rebellion of 66–73, which saw the destruction of the temple in Jerusalem, and the revolt under Bar Kokhba in 132–35, the position of **the Jews** in the Roman Empire was precarious. They had to be seen as loyal and could not risk being confused with Christians. Throughout these years, second-century Judaism was repudiating its links with Second Temple Judaism (with which Christianity had many affinities) and was instead aligning itself with Rabbinic Judaism (see annotated bibliography for *The Religion of the Apostles: Orthodox Christianity in the First Century*).

2. The Romans executed criminals naked, so Polycarp had to **take off all his** *clothes* (but it is unlikely that Jesus was crucified naked, because it was Jewish custom to wear a *loincloth* during executions). **Even before his martyrdom, the faithful** treated him like a saint, **hurrying to** remove **his sandals** in order **to touch his** holy feet (cf. Exod 29:37, 30:29; Lev 6:18, 27/6:11, 20 OSB; 4 Kgdms/2 Kgs 13:20–21; Luke 8:43–48; Matt 28:9; Acts 19:11–12). As a **citizen** of God's heavenly city (Mart Pol 17.1; Phil Sal, 5.2; Phil 3:20), his conduct had been **godly** (literally, *good*).

3. Polycarp's reliance is on the one **who grants**, that is, on the God who graciously deigns to *bestow* his grace. Quite possibly, he did not consider himself worthy to be **nailed** as his Lord had been. **Unmoved** refers first to his body, but also to his spirit. The noble Polycarp will not be **moved** or disturbed (see 5.1 on his not being "disturbed" and Pol 1.1 on his **immovability**).

14

1. So they did not nail him, but bound him instead. Now after he had put his hands behind himself and had, as an outstanding ram out of a great flock, been bound for sacrifice, he was prepared to be a whole burnt offering acceptable to God. He looked up to heaven and said, "O Lord God Almighty, Father of your beloved and blessed Son, Jesus Christ, through whom we have received full knowledge of you, the God of angels and powers and all creation—as well as of the entire race of the righteous who live in your presence:

2. "I bless you because you have counted me worthy of this day and hour to receive a place among the number of the martyrs in the cup of your Christ, and thus to share in the resurrection to eternal life, both of soul and of body, in the incorruptibility of the Holy Spirit. May I be admitted among them in your presence today as a sacrifice that is fat and acceptable, just as you prepared beforehand, showed in advance, and have brought to fulfilment, O never-lying and truthful God.

3. "For this reason, and for all things, I praise you, I bless you, I glorify you through the eternal and heavenly High Priest, Jesus Christ, your beloved Son, through whom be glory to you together with him and the Holy Spirit, both now and unto the ages to come. Amen."

14

1. **Christ** is the lamb Abraham said God would provide (Gen 22:8 MT; cf. the Passover lamb in Exod 12:1–30, John 1:29). Polycarp is like the **ram** Abraham offered **as a whole burnt offering to God** (Gen 22:13, Mart Pol 15.2, Wis 3:1–6). Polycarp **was prepared to be a whole burnt offering** by **being bound** by the Romans and was made **acceptable** by **having bound** himself **to God. Son** also means *Servant* (here and in 14.3, 20.2). Isaiah uses it for Yahweh's Suffering *Servant* (42:1, 49:6, 50:10, 52:13; also see Dem 50–51). Peter and Matthew use it of **Christ** as the **Son** and *Servant* that God sent (Acts 3:13, 26; 4:27, 30; Matt 12:18).

2. Polycarp bears witness before the proconsul to the future **incorruptibility of** the **body**, not just the **soul**, as the Greeks believed. The **sacrifice** being made is that of Polycarp himself, who is drinking **the cup of Christ's** sufferings (Matt 20:22, 26:39–44; 1 Pet 4:13). Polycarp had **fattened** himself by "courage, joy, and grace" to become **an "acceptable sacrifice"** (12.1, 14.1; see Rom 4.1–2 on Ignatius as "**a sacrifice**").What God **prepared beforehand** and **showed in advance** through Polycarp's vision is finally being **brought to fulfilment** (12.3). In calling **God never-lying**, Polycarp may have remembered Ignatius speaking of **Christ** as the Father's "**never-lying** mouth" (Rom 8.2).

3. His **reason** for giving **praise** is his being "counted worthy" to be numbered among "the martyrs" as promised (14.1–2). His prayer is reminiscent of his earlier prayer (Phil 12.2) and of the Great Doxology, a hymn sung before the Divine Liturgy: "We **praise you**, we **bless you**, we worship **you**, we **glorify you**." His closing doxology is his profession of faith, in which he clearly **glorifies** the Trinity and confesses the same to the proconsul. **Unto the ages** is often translated *forever*.

15

1. Now when he had offered up the "Amen" and thus finished his prayer, the men in charge of the fire lit it. And when a great flame blazed forth, we—to whom it was granted to see—saw a miracle. And we were preserved that we might announce to the others what had happened.

2. For the fire, forming the shape of a vaulted chamber, like a ship's sail being filled by wind, completely walled in the body of the martyr. And he was in the middle not like flesh burning, but like bread baking, or like gold and silver glowing in a furnace. For we also encountered a sweet-smelling fragrance so strong that it was like a waft of frankincense or one of the other precious spices.

16

1. Eventually, when the lawless men saw that his body could not be consumed by the fire, they ordered an executioner, who had gone over to him, to stab him with his dagger. And when he did this out came a dove, along with a quantity of blood so large that it put out the fire and caused the entire crowd to marvel that there should be so great a difference between the unbelievers and the elect.

15

1. After the "**Amen**" comes **the fire**. God **granted** the eyewitnesses **to see** the **flame's blazing forth** and the saint's **miraculous preservation** (15.2–16.1). They too were **preserved** from a **fiery** death, unlike the men who had cast the three Hebrew youths into the burning **fiery** furnace (Dan 3:19–22, 46–48 LXX/3:19–22 MT). As a result, they were able to **announce** the good news **to the other** faithful. Literally, **miracle** is *marvel*.

2. The image of a **furnace** brings to mind the three Hebrew youths in the fiery **furnace** who were **not burned** (Dan 3:4–24, 91–94 LXX/3:4–27 MT), while the "blazing flame" from Polycarp's pyre that did not **burn** him (15.1) is like the fire that did not consume the **burning** "bush" (Exod 3:1–4). **Bread baking** reminds one of St. Ignatius's hope to become "pure **bread**" of Christ through martyrdom (Rom 4.1). **Gold** *aglow* **in a furnace** speaks to the refining trials of the Christian (1 Pet 1:6–7). **Precious spices** were often used in embalming to cover up the stench of decay, which was utterly absent in St. Polycarp's case. Instead, there was the *odor of sanctity*, a holy **fragrance** like the **incense** offered at church (cf. Eph 17.1, Mal 1:11, Sir 39:13–14). Such a **sweet** *aroma* as this exuding from a saint has been **encountered** even in our day by many around the world who have received miraculous help from St. Ephraim of Nea Makri (for more on him, see https://www.johnsandopoulos.com/2016/05/saint-ephraim-of-nea-makri-resource-page.html#more).

16

1. The **dagger** used at that time by Roman soldiers had an eleven-inch blade. Just as Jesus was **stabbed** and **out came blood** (John 19:34), so it was with Polycarp. The **dove**, as harbinger of the Spirit, calls to mind the baptism of Christ (John 1:32), except then the **dove came** to usher Christ into his earthly ministry, whereas now **the dove** comes to usher Polycarp into his heavenly reward. **The entire crowd marveled** at how things turned out for God's **elect: the executioner** was preserved, **a dove** just appeared, and a **large** amount **of blood** from a single puncture wound **put out the fire.**

2. This man, the most marvelous Polycarp, was certainly one of them. During our times, he became an apostolic and prophetic teacher as bishop of the Catholic Church at Smyrna. For every utterance that came forth from his mouth was and will be fulfilled.

POLYCARP'S RELICS

17

1. But the jealous and envious and evil one, the adversary of the race of the righteous, when he saw the greatness of Polycarp's martyrdom and his irreproachable citizenship from the start and realized that he had now been crowned with the crown of incorruptibility and had carried off an incontestable prize, took care that not even his poor body should be taken away by us—even though many people were longing to do this and to commune with his dear, holy flesh.

2. So he incited Nicetes, the father of Herod and brother of Alce, to appeal to the magistrate not to give up his body, "lest," he said, "they forsake the Crucified One and begin to worship this man." The Jews, too, were inciting and urging these things. They even kept watch during the time when we were going to take the body from the fire, not understanding that we will never be able either to forsake the Christ—the One who suffered for the salvation of the entire world of those who are being saved, the blameless on behalf of sinners—or worship anyone else.

2. **One of them** means **one of** "the elect" (16.1). **During our times** points to a date for *The Martyrdom of Polycarp* not too long after that of the saint's death in 155 or 156 (21.1, 18.3, 20.1). **Bishop Polycarp**, like Ignatius before him, had the charism of **prophecy** and was **a teacher** of sterling **apostolic** character (Mart Pol 5.2, 12.3, 19.1; Phld 7.2; Tr Sal, 3.1, 3.3; Rom 3.2; Phil 1.1, 8.2, 9.1). According to St. Irenaeus, the charismatic gifts were manifested in **the Catholic Church** throughout the second century (Ag Heresies 2.32.4, 5.6.1). That the **bishop's every utterance** not only **was** but **will be fulfilled** may also indicate a recent martyrdom.

POLYCARP'S RELICS

17

1. **The envious one** is **the one** *who beguiles* (or *bewitches*) *through* **envy** (Tr 4.2; Rom 7.2, 3.1). Polycarp's **irreproachable citizenship** in God's heavenly city began at **the start** of his Christian walk (9.3, 13.2; on his youth, see the Introduction to St. Polycarp). A well-attested alternate reading for **poor body** is *remains*. In English, we call the *remains* of a saint *relics*, a word that comes from the Latin word for *remains* (see Rom 4.2 on St. Ignatius's remains). **Many** of the faithful **were longing to commune with** the *remains* of **his holy** and God-bearing **flesh** (13.2, 17.3). Since that time, **his flesh** has been awaiting the day of its resurrection to **incorruptibility** in the Holy Spirit (14.2, 19.2; Pol 2.3; 4 Macc 17:11–12). The **communion longed** for will soon find further fulfillment when they "gather together" every year "to celebrate" the Eucharist in "commemoration **of his martyrdom**" (18.3).

2. **He** who **incited Nicetes** was "the envious evil one" (17.1). **The Jews** gave this **incitement** support by **urging** the proconsul **not to give up** the martyr's **body**, but rather spread the lie that otherwise the Christians would **worship** Polycarp instead of **"the Crucified One."** **Not understand** can be translated *refuse to* **understand**. Perhaps this **Alce** is the one Ignatius had mentioned (Sm 13.2, Pol 8.3). She may have asked for the saint's **body** and thus prompted a counter**appeal** from **Nicetes**. Just as **the Jews** were involved in **watching** over Polycarp's **body**, so they had been with our Lord's **body** (Matt 27:62–66, 28:4). **Salvation** is *for all the* **world**, not just **the Jews**. **Being saved** involves one's whole lifetime (1 Cor 1:18, Phil 2:12, 2 Cor 1:6).

3. For we worship this One, because he is the Son of God, while the martyrs, as disciples and imitators of the Lord, we love in a manner worthy of them on account of their matchless affection for their very own King and Teacher. May it be granted even to us to become their fellow partakers, as well as their fellow disciples.

18

1. Therefore, when the centurion saw the contentiousness exhibited by the Jews, he placed the body in the middle, as was their custom, and burned it.

2. Consequently, it was later on that we took up his bones, more precious than costly jewels and more valuable than pure gold, and deposited them in a place that was indeed appropriate.

3. There, when we gather together as we can with gladness and joy, the Lord will permit us to celebrate the birthday of his martyrdom, both for the commemoration of the athletes of earlier contests and also for the training and the preparation of those yet to compete.

3. The faithful of Smyrna **worship** Christ alone, for **he is the Son of God** who "suffered for" our "salvation" (17.2). **But** they also have **love** for his **martyrs**, who shed their blood for him. **Affection** is an admirable quality of **imitators**. **To** be **fellow partakers** (or *communers*) and "to commune with" Polycarp's "dear, holy flesh" (17.1) are part of what the Apostles's Creed calls "the *communion* of saints." Saints are people or things that have been sanctified, made holy, by intimate contact with the holy (13.2, Eph 2.2).

18

1. **The Jews** had been **contending** for **the body** (17.1-2) in order to **burn it** (13.1). They did not use cremation for themselves, but had a **custom** of doing so with perpetrators of heinous crimes against God (12.2, Lev 20:14, Josh 8:28/8:26 OSB). So **the centurion burned the body in the middle** of the relit funeral pyre.

2. With what affection do these Christians take up the **bones** of the venerable Polycarp, with what care do they find an **appropriate place** for burial, and with what tenderness do they **deposit** their **precious** treasure.

3. **There** is where his "bones" are (18.2). This is the first record of a Eucharist being **celebrated** on a saint's deathday as his heavenly **birthday** (see Rom 6.1 on Ignatius's **martyrdom** as a **birth**; on **gather together**, see Eph 5.3, 13.1, 20.2). This **celebration** is to occur on the first anniversary of the **martyrdom** of Polycarp, who was "a perfect **athlete**" in his **contest** (Pol 1.3, 2.3, 3.1; Phil 9.1). **When we gather** sounds like such a **commemoration** is already their practice. **Earlier contestants** include the eleven others "martyred at Smyrna" (19.1, 2.2-4). **Training** can be translated *ascetical exercise* or *practice* (Mag 1.1, Pol 1.3, Phil 9.1).

CONCLUSION, INSTRUCTIONS, AND FAREWELL

19

1. Such are the events concerning the blessed Polycarp. Including those from Philadelphia, he was the twelfth person to be martyred at Smyrna. He alone is especially remembered by all, so that he is spoken of everywhere, even by the pagans. Not only did he prove to be an outstanding teacher, but also an eminent martyr. All long to imitate his martyrdom, since it took place in accordance with the gospel of Christ.

2. Through his patient endurance he overcame the unrighteous ruler, and thus obtained the crown of incorruptibility. Rejoicing with the apostles and all the righteous, he is glorifying the Almighty God and Father and blessing our Lord Jesus Christ, the Savior of our souls and Pilot of our bodies and Shepherd of the Catholic Church throughout the inhabited world.

20

1. You did indeed request that the events be explained to you at length. We, however, for the present, have made them known in somewhat of a summary through our brother Marcion. Once you have learned about these things, you are to send this epistle to the brothers and sisters farther on, that they too may glorify the Lord, who makes his choices from among his own servants.

2. Now to him who is able to bring us all by his grace and bounty into his eternal kingdom through his Son, the only-begotten Jesus Christ, be glory, honor, might, and majesty unto the ages. Greet all the saints. Those with us greet you, as does Evarestus, who wrote this, along with his whole household.

CONCLUSION, INSTRUCTIONS, AND FAREWELL

19

1. The **martyrdom** of **the blessed Polycarp** brought the number of **martyrs** from **Philadelphia** and **Smyrna** up to **twelve**, one of which was Germanicus (3.1). The **Philadelphians** had "rejoice[d] in the passion of our Lord without wavering" (Phld Sal). Now some of them have made **Christ's** "passion" their "passion" (Sm 4.2). Yet only Polycarp was **remembered by** both **pagans** and Christians—and especially the latter, for they deemed **his martyrdom** worthy of **imitation since it took place "in accordance with the gospel"** (1.1).

2. The **unrighteous ruler** is the devil. Polycarp has "**endured** to the end" and "been **saved**," just as **Jesus** said would happen (Matt 24:13). He has now rejoined **the apostles**, who are **rejoicing** in his "triumph" (Pol 3.1), and is awaiting the resurrection when he will receive the "prize" of "**incorruptibility**" for faithfully "**piloting**" the **church** at Smyrna (Pol 2.3, Mart Pol 14.2). At that time may **our Lord crown** us as well.

20

1. **We** indicates a community collaboration (cf. 15.1). **Marcion** may have been the author, a witness, the courier, or some combination, but not the amanuensis (20.2) or arch-heretic (on whom, see Phil 7.1; Mart Pol Mosc 22.3; Polycarp Intro, 159, fnn. 21–23). By saying **to send this epistle to the** believers **farther on** (Phld 10.1, Sm 11.1, Pol 7.2, Phil 13.2), the author shows he is writing shortly after Polycarp's martyrdom when the news had not yet spread. The **choices** for martyrdom should belong to **the Lord** (1.2, 2.1, 3.1). Quintus's reckless decision to be a martyr was a violation of this (4.1). While some martyrs under the Ottoman yoke did **choose** to be martyred, they did not do so rashly, but only with their spiritual father's blessing.

2. The author now gives **glory** to God for his unique *Servant* and **Son, Jesus Christ** (the same Greek word that can be translated *Servant* and **Son** is found in 14.1, 3; 1 Clem 59.2, 3, 4; Did 9.22, 10.2, 10.3; Diogn 8.9, 8.11, 9.1). We are **all saints** and are to become **saints**. **Evarestus** was the amanuensis **who wrote** for the author, just as Tertius had done for St. Paul (Rom 16:22).

EARLY ADDITION

21

1. Now the blessed Polycarp bore witness by being martyred on the second day of the first part of the month of Xanthicus, seven days before the kalends of March, on a special Sabbath, at the eighth hour. And his arrest by Herod took place during the high priesthood of Philip of Tralles, while Statius Quadratus was serving as proconsul, but Jesus Christ was reigning as King unto the ages. To him be the glory, honor, majesty, and eternal throne from generation unto generation. Amen.

EARLY ADDITION

21

1. This addition may have been an original supplement, but it seems more likely to be an early addendum. The translation **bore witness by being martyred** includes both meanings of the same verb (so also in 1.1, 22.1). The date was *February 23*, which the text gives according to the Macedonian and Roman calendars. Every year on this date the Orthodox Church commemorates St. Polycarp's life and **martyrdom**. The most likely date for his death is *February 23, 155*, which was a Saturday, a **Sabbath** (see Polycarp Intro, 160, fn. 26; for more on **special Sabbath**, see 8.1, 13.1). The time was *2:00 p.m.* (**the eighth hour**). Roman dating included the names of officials in office and ended with the name of the emperor. Here the author leaves out the name of the emperor and concludes with **Jesus Christ reigning** on his **eternal throne as King unto the ages**.

LATER ADDITIONS

22

1. We wish that you all may fare well, brothers and sisters, as you walk by the word of Jesus Christ that is in accordance with the gospel. With him be glory to the God and Father and the Holy Spirit for the salvation of the holy elect. In this way the blessed Polycarp walked when he bore witness by being martyred. May it be granted us to be found following in his footsteps in the kingdom of Jesus Christ.

2. Gaius copied this account from the papers of Irenaeus, a disciple of Polycarp. He had also lived together in the same city with Irenaeus. And I, Socrates, wrote it out in Corinth from the copies of Gaius. Grace be with everyone.

LATER ADDITIONS

22

1. The material found here as 22.1 is not found in the Moscow Manuscript. The church at Philomelium, which was the recipient of *The Martyrdom of Polycarp* (1.1), may have added this section as a kind of postscript before "sending the epistle to" those "farther on" (20.1). The phrase **in accordance with the gospel** harks back to 1.1 and 19.1 and refers to **Polycarp's martyrdom**. This **word of Jesus Christ** is found in "**the** fourfold **gospel**" of the Evangelists (Ag Heresies 3.11.7–9, Phil 12.1) and is opposed to "an[y] other **gospel**" (Gal 1:6–7). The phrase **the God and Father** is a common one (19.2; Phil 12.2; 2 Cor 1:3, 11:31; Eph 5:20; Col 1:3; 1 Thess 1:3, 3:11; 2 Thess 2:16; Jas 1:27; 1 Pet 1:3; four times in the Anaphora of the Liturgy of St. Basil). **Christ** may be referred to as **God** (for examples of **Christ** as **God**, see Eph Sal, 1.1, 18.2; Rom 3.3, 6.3; Sm 1.1; Pol 8.3), but the **Father** is called **the God**. This is seen especially in John 1:1–2, which literally reads, "In the beginning was the Word, and the Word was with **the God**, and the Word was **God**. The Same One was in the beginning with **the God**." In the Nicene Creed, "the Lord **Jesus Christ**" is literally called "the only begotten Son of **the God**." As **Polycarp** gave **glory** to the Trinity (14.3), so too does the author here. **Christ's kingdom** is for those who continue to **walk by** this **word** (or *message*) **in** the **footsteps** of **Polycarp**, who died to himself and the world for **Jesus Christ** (Gal 5:24, 6:14; Rom 7.2; for what Ignatius says about Paul's **footsteps**, see Eph 12.2). May "the Lord's mercy" **be found** "**following**" us until we "settle down in" his "house" at the completion of our sojourn (Ps 22/23:6).

2. St. **Irenaeus** was **a disciple of** St. **Polycarp**, who had been **a disciple of** the Apostle John. The word **he** refers to **Gaius**, not **Polycarp**, as residing **in the same city with Irenaeus**. The benediction—**Grace be with everyone**—appears to come from **Socrates**.

3. And I, Pionius, wrote it out again from the manuscript mentioned above, after searching for it based on the blessed Polycarp's revelation when he appeared to me, as I will explain in what follows. And I gathered it together when nearly worn away by time, in order that the Lord Jesus Christ might gather me also with his elect into his heavenly kingdom. To him be the glory together with the Father and the Holy Spirit unto the ages of the ages. Amen.

LATER ADDITIONS ACCORDING TO
THE MOSCOW MANUSCRIPT

22

1. Gaius copied this account from the papers of Irenaeus. He had also lived together in the same city with Irenaeus, who had been a disciple of the holy Polycarp.

3. The history of the transmission of *The Martyrdom of Polycarp* (as delineated in 22.2–3 and Mosc 22.1–5) begins when records of the account are passed down from **Polycarp's** disciple, Irenaeus, to his contemporary, Gaius, while they are in Rome. In Corinth, Socrates (or Isocrates) writes out Gaius's copies. Finally, **blessed Polycarp reveals to Pionius** the location of Socrates's **manuscript**, which he then **gathers together**. Later, as a presbyter in Smyrna, St. **Pionius** will be arrested on the anniversary of St. **Polycarp's** death, February 23, and martyred on March 11, 250. The fourth-century *Life of Polycarp* (cited in the comments on 6.1) claims to be by the same **Pionius** (see Polycarp Intro, 158, fn. 13). Although viewed unfavorably by most scholars, some of its information can be found in the *Synaxarion* and *The Prologue from Ochrid*.

LATER ADDITIONS ACCORDING TO THE MOSCOW MANUSCRIPT

22

1. This conclusion is from Codex Mosquensis 159 and may have been written in the third or fourth century. This translation follows a more traditional numbering for the sections in this manuscript than Holmes and Hartog do. Here (and in Mart Pol Mosc 22.3), **Polycarp** is called **holy**, rather than "blessed" (Phil 3.2).

2. For this Irenaeus was in Rome teaching many at the time of the martyrdom of Bishop Polycarp. And many most excellent and sound writings of his are in circulation. In these he recalled Polycarp, saying that he had learned from him as his disciple. And he ably refuted every heresy and handed down the ecclesiastical and catholic rule just as he had received it from the saint.

3. And he also says this, that Marcion, after whom the Marcionites are named, once met the holy Polycarp and said, "Recognize us, Polycarp." And he said to Marcion, "I do recognize you. I recognize the firstborn of Satan!"

2. **Refuted** brings to mind the title of **Irenaeus's** major work, *Refutation and Overthrow of Knowledge Falsely So-Called*, commonly called *Against Heresies*. Our sources show three times when **Irenaeus** mentioned **Polycarp** (Ag Heresies 3.3.4; his *Epistle to Florinus*, found in Ch Hist 5.20.4–8; and his *Epistle to Victor*, found in Ch Hist 5.24.11–18). **The ecclesiastical and catholic rule** is the *Church's universally-held* **rule** or *standard* of faith or truth. Literally, **rule** is *a ruler*, as in a *straight edge* that ensures strict alignment with what is *right*. The underlying Greek word is often transliterated as *canon*. For Irenaeus, this **rule** is a hermeneutical framework for summarizing and demarcating *the Church's* true faith in the revelation of the one God, the Father, and the one Lord, Jesus Christ, his Son and Word, who made all things with the Father, became true man and dwelt among us, teaching and working miracles, and was crucified and raised from the dead for our salvation "according to the" Old Testament "scriptures" (1 Cor 15:3, 4; the Nicene Creed; Ag Heresies 3.18.3), in which he was foretold by the Spirit, by whom we have rebirth in baptism. Our Lord was revealed in the Church through his cross-bearing apostles by their preaching, miracles, way of life, and **writings**. Their Gospels and Epistles were **handed down** to their successors in what came to be called the *canon* of the New Testament. We have several passages from Irenaeus that lay out various elements of **the rule** (Ag Heresies 1.10.1, 3.4.2; Dem 3, 6; also see the statements of Ignatius in Sm 1.1–2). Clement of Alexandria succinctly describes "**the ecclesiastical rule**" as "the symphony and harmony of the Law and the Prophets in the covenant **handed down** at the coming of the Lord" (Misc 6.15.125.3).

3. **Marcion** was a second-century arch-heretic who blasphemed the God of the Old Testament as a malevolent being who was not the loving Father of our Lord Jesus Christ. This required him to mutilate *The Gospel according to Luke* and the ten Pauline epistles that he accepted, because otherwise these would not agree with him. **He** refers to St. Irenaeus, who recorded the story recounted here (Ag Heresies 3.3.4). When **Marcion** said, "**Recognize us**," he meant, "*Acknowledge us as legitimate* before God." **Polycarp**, however, used "**recognize** to mean, "**I do** *notice* who you really are. I *acknowledge that you are* **Satan's** *legitimate* **firstborn!**" Prior to this, Polycarp had used the phrase "**firstborn of Satan**" to refer to the Docetists (Phil 7.1).

4. And this also is brought out in the writings of Irenaeus, that on the day and at the hour in Smyrna when Polycarp was martyred, Irenaeus was in the city of Rome and heard a voice like a trumpet saying, "Polycarp has been martyred."

5. So Gaius copied this account from the writings of Irenaeus, as was stated above. And from the copy of Gaius, Isocrates in Corinth made a copy. And I, Pionius, wrote it out again from the copy of Isocrates after searching for it based on the revelation of the holy Polycarp. And I gathered it together when nearly worn away by time, in order that the Lord Jesus Christ might gather me also with his elect into his heavenly kingdom. To him be the glory together with the Father and the Son and the Holy Spirit unto the ages of the ages. Amen.

4. Earlier, when entering the stadium, **Polycarp** himself had heard a heavenly **voice** (9.1). Now, when **Polycarp** departs as a victorious **martyr, Irenaeus hears a voice like a trumpet**. In the future, the sound of **a trumpet** will be heard throughout the world when the faithful are gathered up to be with their Lord at his second coming (Matt 24:30–31, 1 Thess 4:16, 1 Cor 15:52). The information found in **this** section is not contained **in** any of **the writings of Irenaeus** that we possess.

5. The Moscow manuscript's conclusion reads **Isocrates**, rather than Socrates (as in 22.2). There is a tradition that this **Isocrates**, after he had visited all the philosophical schools, heard a voice directing him to Christianity. Subsequently, he traveled to Smyrna, where he found and entered the Catholic Church. At first glance, the Trinitarian doxology appears faulty, as if it refers to four persons, instead of three (as the parallel doxology in 22.3 clearly does). One might expect **To him** to point back to **the Lord Jesus Christ**, but that would make **and the Son** redundant. It is more likely that the author meant what he wrote, and most unlikely that he mistakenly added **and the Son**. So **to him** should be taken to refer to **St. Polycarp**, the subject of this epistle, whom God has **glorified** (on **glorified**, see Eph 2.2, Phld 10.2, John 7:39, 2 Thess 2:14, Ag Heresies 4.38.3, and the Kontakion for *St.* Polycarp, which can be found above on the last page of the Introduction to *St.* Polycarp). Let us say, then, with *St.* **Polycarp** and *St.* Ignatius and all the **glorified** martyrs throughout **the ages: Glory be to the Father and to the Son and to the Holy Spirit unto the ages of the ages. Amen.**

For Further Reading

Most of the works that follow include bibliographical information. However, publication details may be omitted where the original writings were in Greek or Latin and translations are now available online and in print. If a work cited in footnotes is not included below, it can be found online.

Against Heresies. Irenaeus. Available online and in print. Late second century.
Five-volume refutation of the Gnostic heresies. Fragments of his lost writings are sometimes included.

The Ancestral Sin. John S. Romanides. Ridgewood, NJ: Zephyr, 2002.
Orthodox exposition of redemption as found in St. Ignatius and other church fathers of the first two centuries down to St. Irenaeus.

The Apostolic Fathers.
Title given to those men who came after the apostles, like Ignatius and Polycarp. Their writings are from the late first to mid-second century. Particular translations of these writings are annotated in the next two entries.

The Apostolic Fathers: Greek texts and English translations. 3rd ed. Michael W. Holmes. Grand Rapids: Baker Academic, 2007.
Holmes's Greek and Latin texts for St. Ignatius and St. Polycarp are the ones usually followed in this translation. His texts and translations are revisions of J. B. Lightfoot's seminal work.

The Apostolic Fathers: Volume 4, Ignatius of Antioch. Robert M. Grant. Camden, N.J: Thomas Nelson & Sons, 1966.
Superb translation with short commentary.

Apostolic Succession. Gregory Rogers. Mount Hermon, CA: Conciliar, 1989. Concise booklet on the biblical foundation and historic evidence for apostolic succession.

Bearing God: The Life and Work of St. Ignatius of Antioch the God-Bearer. Andrew Stephen Damick. Chesterton, IN: Ancient Faith, 2017. Edifying treatment of St. Ignatius's life and concerns: martyrdom, salvation in Christ, the bishop, the unity of the Church, and the Eucharist.

Church History. Eusebius. Available online and in print. Fourth century. First history of the Church after *The Acts of the Apostles*. Covers from Christ to Constantine.

Dialogue with Trypho. Justin Martyr. Available online and in print. Mid-second century. Dialogue between St. Justin and a Jew that defends Christ and the Church as the fulfillment of Old Testament prophecy. Gives insight into approaches to scripture that may have been employed by St. Ignatius's Judaizing opponents in Magnesia and Philadelphia.

From the Lost Teaching of Polycarp. Charles E. Hill. Tübingen: Mohr Siebeck, 2006. Perceptive study on St. Polycarp as St. Irenaeus's "apostolic presbyter" in *Against Heresies* and as the author of the *Epistle to Diognetus*.

The Holy Bible. Athens: The Zoe Brotherhood of Theologians, 1928. Greek-only text used by the Church of Greece.

Ignatius of Antioch. William R. Schoedel. Hermeneia. Philadelphia: Fortress, 1985. Sound translation with academic commentary.

Irenaeus of Lyons: Identifying Christianity. John Behr. Oxford: Oxford University Press, 2013. Exceptional introduction to St. Irenaeus and his major work *Against Heresies*.

Irenaeus on the Christian Faith: A Condensation of Against Heresies. James R. Payton, Jr. Eugene, OR: Pickwick, 2011.
A good abridgement in modern English of the Ante-Nicene Fathers translation that is readily available online and in print. Briefly covers Books 1 and 2 on Gnostic teachings; then focuses on the teaching of Christ and his apostles in Books 3–5.

Jesus the Messiah in the Hebrew Bible. Eugen J. Pentiuc. New York/Mahwah, N.J: Paulist, 2006.
Scholarly, yet pious, handling of the Old Testament messianic prophecies as they are found in the MT, the LXX, the Aramaic Targumim, and the New Testament. Relevant to the disagreements between Ignatius and his Judaizing opponents in Magnesia and Philadelphia.

Learning Christ: Ignatius of Antioch and the Mystery of Redemption. Gregory Vall. Washington, DC: The Catholic University of America Press, 2013.
Powerful reflection on the mystery of redemption based on a historically-informed exegesis of the seven epistles of St. Ignatius.

Martyrdom and Persecution in the Early Church. W. H. C. Frend. Grand Rapids, MI: Anchor, 1965. Reprinted, 1967.
Classic treatment of this topic.

The Martyrdom of Ignatius. Available online and in print. Possibly written down in the fourth century.
Written account of St. Ignatius's martyrdom. Contains important oral traditions.

The Mystery of Christ: Life in Death. John Behr. Crestwood, N.Y: St. Vladimir's Seminary Press, 2006.
Brilliant reflection on the mystery of Christ as learned by the apostles through their experience of the cross, and then revealed to others through their lives and writings and the leaders who followed them, including Ignatius and Irenaeus.

The Mystical Theology of the Eastern Church. Vladimir Lossky. Translated by the Fellowship of St. Alban and St. Sergius. Cambridge: James Clark & Co. Ltd., 1957. Reprinted, 1973.
Vintage treatment of the Eastern Orthodox way of knowing God as distinct from western Catholic and Protestant approaches.

A New English Translation of the Septuagint. 2nd printing. Oxford: Oxford University Press, 2009.
Academic translation—with useful introductory information on translation issues—of each book of the Old Testament. Frequently consulted for this book. (Available online at https://ccat.sas.upenn.edu/nets/edition/)

On the Apostolic Preaching. John Behr. Crestwood, NY: St. Vladimir's Seminary Press, 1997.
Scholarly translation with notes on Irenaeus's late-second century *Demonstration of the Apostolic Preaching.* Uses Old Testament prophecies to expound the apostolic message. Complements Justin Martyr's *Dialogue with Trypho.*

The Orthodox Church. New ed. Timothy (Kallistos) Ware. New York: Penguin, 1997.
The premier introduction to the history, faith, and worship of the Orthodox Church.

Orthodox Spirituality. 2nd ed. A Monk of the Eastern Church. Crestwood, NY: St. Vladimir's Seminary Press, 1996.
Short, sublime introduction to the first principles of Orthodox spirituality.

Orthodox Study Bible. Nashville, TN: Thomas Nelson, 2008.
Translation of the Greek Old Testament (LXX) and the Greek New Testament with comments and other study aids.

Polycarp, a destroyer of our gods. Rick Lambert. Mason, OH: Landbright, 2014.
Historical novel that illustrates Polycarp's discipling of church leaders and influence on the formation of the New Testament canon.

Polycarp and Paul: An Analysis of Their Literary and Theological Relationship in Light of Polycarp's Use of Biblical and Extra-Biblical Literature. VC Supplement 62. Kenneth Berding. Leiden: Brill, 2002.
Thorough study of Polycarp's use of Paul's epistles and theology and his imitation of Paul.

Polycarp's Epistle to the Philippians and the Martyrdom of Polycarp. Paul Hartog. Oxford: Oxford University Press, 2013.
Excellent introduction, text, translation, and commentary on both writings. Frequently consulted for this book.

The Prologue from Ochrid. Bishop Nikolai Velimirović. Birmingham, UK: Lazarica, 1985.
Inspiring Orthodox collection of the Lives of the Saints.

The Religion of the Apostles: Orthodox Christianity in the First Century. Stephen De Young. Chesterton, IN: Ancient Faith, 2021.
Study that demonstrates how Orthodox Christian beliefs and practices appeared in the first century as the continuation and fulfilment of Second Temple Judaism, rather than as the result of later, centuries-long developments.

Septuaginta, A Reader's Edition. Gregory R. Lanier and William A. Ross, eds. Peabody, MA: Hendrickson, 2018.
Makes reading the Septuagint a joy with its accessible vocabulary and parsing. Uses the Septuagint text edited by Alfred Rahlfs and revised by Robert Hanhart.

Springtime of the Liturgy, Liturgical Texts of the First Four Centuries. Lucien Deiss. Collegeville, MN: The Liturgical Press, 1979.
Fine annotated collection from Jewish prayers to the *Catechesis* of St. Cyril of Jerusalem.

The Synaxarion of Holy Hieromartyr Ignatius, the God Bearer of Antioch. December 20. Available online and in print.
The life of St. Ignatius that is read in public worship in the Orthodox Church.

The Synaxarion of Holy Hieromartyr Polycarp, the Bishop of Smyrna. February 23. Available online and in print.
The life of St. Polycarp that is read in public worship in the Orthodox Church.

Two Epistles of St. Patrick the Bishop. Patricia Colling Egan. Maysville, MO: St. Nicholas, 2020.
Groundbreaking translation of his *Confession* and *Letter to the Soldiers of Coroticus.*

Unseen Warfare. Lorenzo Scupoli. Edited by St. Nicodemus of the Holy Mountain. Revised by St. Theophan the Recluse. Translated by E. Kadloubovsky and G. E. H. Palmer. Crestwood, NY: St. Vladimir's Seminary Press, 1987.
Penetrating spiritual classic that combines insights from the West and the East on the conflict that occurs in the arena of our hearts.

The Way of the Warrior Saint: How to Live a Crucifixional Life. Fr. Christopher Salamy. Bloomington, IN: WestBow, 2021.
Practical and humorous how-to book that addresses life's challenges with helpful stories and tips for living a life of self-sacrifice.

About the Author

WILLIAM W. WEBER HOLDS a BA in History from Asbury University and an MA in History from the University of Kentucky. He wrote his thesis on Irenaeus's understanding of the relationship between the Old and New Covenants in the light of his polemic against the Gnostics. He and his wife Lindsey raised five children and have five grandchildren. They became members of the Orthodox Church in 1990. Subsequently, William earned the St. Stephen's Certificate in Orthodox Theology and was ordained sub-deacon. From 1980 to his retirement in 2020, he worked in banking and insurance, served as an administrator in Christian colleges—including Rose Hill, an Orthodox Great Books college—and taught history in high school and college. William and Lindsey are members of St. Michael Orthodox Church in Louisville, Kentucky, where they serve as church school teachers. Together they have published articles on the loss of their son, Joseph, and their subsequent pilgrimages to Greece. William's presentations on Dostoevsky and Byzantium may be heard online. Besides teaching, he and his wife usher, welcome visitors, serve as Godparents, and help at a new mission. William may be reached at divineeconomy@proton.me.

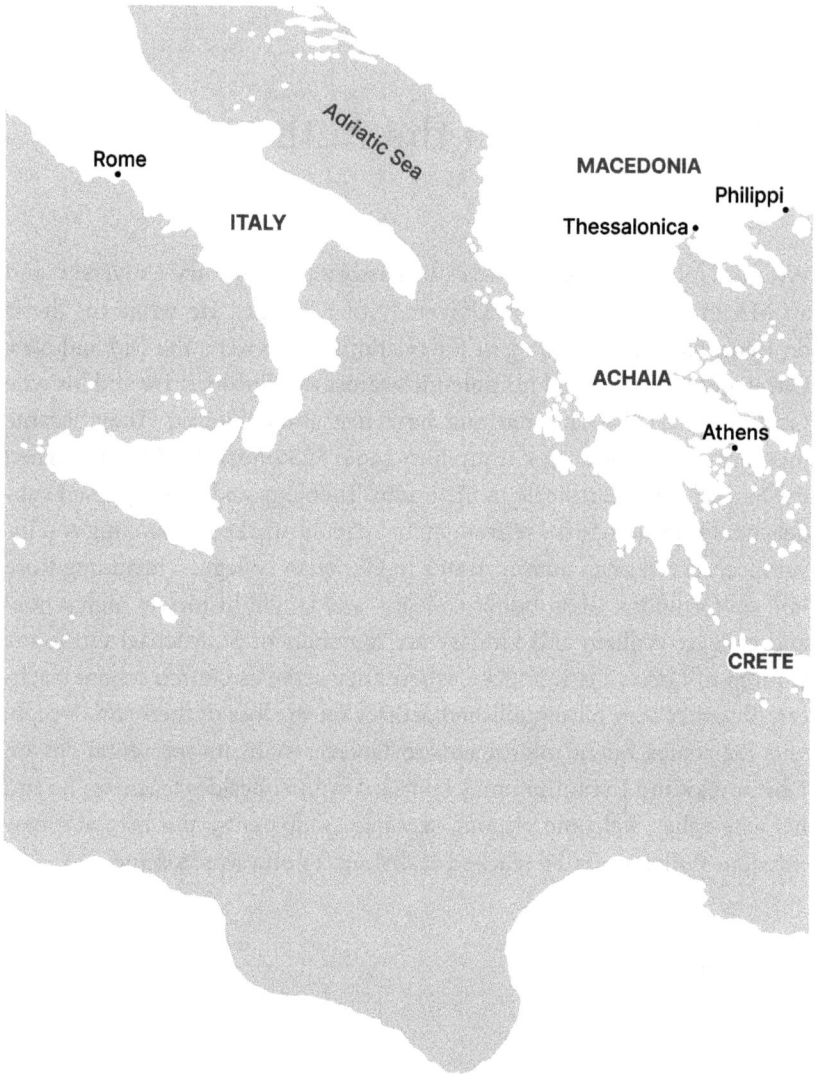

Rome

ITALY

Adriatic Sea

MACEDONIA

Philippi

Thessalonica

ACHAIA

Athens

CRETE

The World of St. Ignatius

and St. Polycarp

Become more eager
in exerting effort
than you are.
Carefully notice
opportunities.

St. Ignatius of Antioch
The Epistle to St. Polycarp 3.2

We wish that you all may fare well,
brothers and sisters,
as you walk by the word of Jesus Christ
that is in accordance with the gospel.
With him be glory to the God and Father
and the Holy Spirit
for the salvation of the holy elect.
In this way the blessed Polycarp walked
when he bore witness
by being martyred.
May it be granted us to be found
following in his footsteps
in the kingdom of Jesus Christ.

The Martyrdom of St. Polycarp 22.1

www.ingramcontent.com/pod-product-compliance
Lightning Source LLC
Chambersburg PA
CBHW060331100426
42812CB00003B/952